'Izagirre brings to life the Cerro Rico, its history and the people who work its seams. Clear-sighted and unsentimental, yet burning with a quiet power and rage, *The Mountain that Eats Men* will move you to tears and to anger.'
Mark Mann, author of *The Gringo Trail*

'A gut-puncher of a book. A powerful, important work that puts the human back into human rights.'
Oliver Balch, author of *Viva South America!*

'Explores the fascinating and tragic story of the exploitation of Potosí, one of the richest deposits of silver and tin on the planet. Izagirre's narrative of characters eking out a living amidst what, for many, ultimately became silver-lined tombs is deft, admirable, and haunting.'
Kim MacQuarrie, author of *Life and Death In the Andes*

'Izagirre uses what appears to be a small, personal story to tell a much wider, more universal one. Like Kapuściński, he finds the drop of water that reflects everything around it.'
El País

'Izagirre … is an old-style reporter in terms of his exquisite technique and his professionalism, but also a journalist of the 21st century when it comes to the risks he takes, his incredible commitment, his irony and his humour.'
El Descodificador

'Shares the spirit of Eduardo Galeano – and also of Naomi Klein's Shock Doctrine. But Izagirre gets closer to the ground.'
Culturamas

The Mountain that Eats Men

ANDER IZAGIRRE

TRANSLATED BY TIM GUTTERIDGE

Supported using public funding by
**ARTS COUNCIL
ENGLAND**

This edition of *The Mountain that Eats Men* was published in 2019 by Zed Books Ltd, The Foundry, 17 Oval Way, London SE11 5RR, UK.

www.zedbooks.net

English language translation © Tim Gutteridge 2018

Copyright © Ander Izagirre 2017

Originally published in Spanish by Libros del KO in 2017.

This translation is published by arrangement with Oh! Books Agencia Literaria.

This book has been selected to receive financial assistance from English PEN's "PEN Translates" programme, supported by Arts Council England. English PEN exists to promote literature and our understanding of it, to uphold writers' freedoms around the world, to campaign against the persecution and imprisonment of writers for stating their views, and to promote the friendly co-operation of writers and the free exchange of ideas. www.englishpen.org

The right of Ander Izagirre to be identified as the author of this work has been asserted by him in accordance with the Copyright, Designs and Patents Act, 1988.

Typeset in Sabon by seagulls.net
Cover design by Steve Leard

A catalogue record for this book is available from the British Library

ISBN 978-1-78699-455-4 pb
ISBN 978-1-78699-457-8 pdf
ISBN 978-1-78699-458-5 epub
ISBN 978-1-78699-459-2 mobi

Printed by CPI Group (UK) Ltd, Croydon CR0 4YY

CONTENTS

ACKNOWLEDGEMENTS

Daniel Burgui is one of the most important people in this book, even if this is his only appearance. He was my travelling companion on my first trip to Bolivia and on other projects in the country over many years, and we shared discoveries, excitement, sadness, the occasional disappointment – and a never-ending list of debts. Dani is generous, sensitive and cheerful. He is also a journalist from whom I have learned a great deal: because he is a wonderful writer; because he treats people with great respect; because he accompanies them before, during and afterwards; and because he always comes back. And he's a great friend – who always come back.

I owe a huge debt of thanks to the people who live on Cerro Rico de Potosí and in the mining district of Llallagua, for giving me their time and their knowledge, and for welcoming me into their lives. Some of them appear in this book and others do not (or at least not with their real names). They are guards and *palliris*, miners and watchmen, teachers and administrators, girls and boys.

I also want to express my thanks to Miguel Sánchez-Ostiz for giving me the first – excellent – clues that set me on the trail to Bolivia.

And to Cecilia Molina, Héctor Soliz, Maxime Chiquet, José Pimentel, Dora Camacho, Modesto Pérez, Fernando Pérez, Gary Daher and Ramón Rocha Monroy, for giving me their time and acting as my guides in Bolivia, enabling me to gain a deeper understanding of the country and of the history of the mines. I would also like to express my thanks for the assistance I received from the staff of Cepromin and Voces Libres, and to state my admiration for their commitment.

To Álex Ayala Ugarte and Karim Patón, for their hospitality and all the good times we've shared.

To Eider Elizegi, for her companionship on the road and for her insightful observations in Bolivia.

To all the other friends, family and strangers who contributed to the Escuela Robertito project in Cerro Rico.

While writing this book, I was privileged to receive some very special support, with my text being read and commented on by Martín Caparrós, Eileen Truax, Roberto Valencia, Catalina Lobo-Guerrero, Andrés Wiesner, Claudia Jardim, Esteban Castro, Cecilia Lanza and Diego Fonseca. We spent a week together in Oaxaca (Mexico), at a workshop organized by Fundación Nuevo Periodismo Iberoamericano, working under the brilliant guidance of Caparrós on our blocked writing projects. Without their help, this book would be far weaker; even with their help, there are plenty of shortcomings which they identified but I was unable to fix.

I would also like to thank Jaime Martín, June Fernández, Nerea Armendáriz and Sara Agnetti for reading, discussing and commenting on the book in some detail. They had the great literary virtue of enabling me to see a solution – and to identify a hundred new problems.

Finally, it is with great fondness that I remember Gregorio Iriarte, who died in Cochabamba from a cause he would never have predicted: old age.

In The Land of Fabulous Treasures

'A woman can't enter the mine,' Pedro Villca tells me. 'Can you imagine? The woman has her period and Pachamama gets jealous. Then Pachamama hides the ore and the seam disappears.'

Villca is an old miner, an unlikely combination in Bolivia. He's fifty-nine and none of his comrades have made it to his age. He's alive, he says, because he was never greedy. Most miners work for months or even years without a break. Most miners end up working twenty-four-hour shifts, fuelled by coca leaves and liquor, a practice for which they have invented a verb, *veinticuatrear*: 'to twen-ty-four'. Instead he would come up to the surface, go back to his parents' village for a few months to grow potatoes and herd llamas, fill his lungs with clean air to flush the dust out of them, and then go back to the mine. But he was never there when his companions were asphyxiated by a pocket of gas or crushed by a rockfall. He knows he's already taken too many chances with death and that he shouldn't push his luck. So he's decided to retire. He swears that in a few weeks' time he'll retire.

Villca is barely five feet tall. Even so, he has to crouch down to avoid banging his helmet on the eucalyptus beams that hold up the gallery. He walks bent almost double and with his arms pinned to his sides because in this tiny tunnel ...

'This damn wormhole!'

... because in this tunnel if you flex your arms they brush against the walls on either side, and if you raise your head your helmet bangs against the roof. We're inside a mountain. There are a few inches of air around our bodies and, beyond that, millions of tons of solid rock. It's as close as you can get to being buried alive. This wormhole is the only way back to the surface, as long as you know how to find your way through the labyrinth of snaking, crossing, forking, twisting, rising, falling galleries. There's nothing in the tunnels, in the caves, in the shafts – no light, no breeze, no sound – to indicate if we are heading back towards life or down into the depths of the mountain. It is as if a single sneeze would be enough to make the mountain contract and crush this gallery as we feel our way along it like two insects, touching the walls, walking with our feet and with our hands.

It's hard to breathe. In this position, crouching, with our arms held rigidly at our sides, our lungs can't expand fully. Each intake of breath requires conscious effort: I flare my nostrils and pull in air that is stiflingly hot, saturated with humidity, sticky like cotton wool soaked in turpentine. It leaves a metallic taste on my tongue as if I've been sucking coins. It's *copajira*, the acidic sweat of the mine that floats in the air and trickles down the walls, forming puddles of orange mud.

Villca is in his element. He's enjoying himself. He tells me to sit down for a moment and switch off the torch on my helmet. Then he turns off his own. As soon as I hear the click, darkness falls like a flood, like a black wave that washes me down the gallery into the depths of the mountain. I haven't moved but I feel movement nonetheless. A wave of dizziness crashes against my brain, I lose my balance, my ears are buzzing. I observe a stoical silence because that bastard Villca is laughing. I breathe deeply and I can feel my carotid artery pulsing in my neck.

'Fuck.'

'Turn it back on,' he says.

I turn on the torch and look at Villca, and his long shadow is projected against the roof, stretched out tall across the beams. He smiles.

'And those beams?' I ask. They're rotten, buckled into a V-shape by the weight of the mountain; some of them have already started to splinter.

'*Callapos*. Thirty years since they were replaced, the bastards. Nobody has money to invest in safety, the mining gangs are small, we barely make enough to survive. We work the find, pray it doesn't fall in, then look for another one.'

He keeps going. He's agile, despite his fifty-nine years. He bends down, stands up, crawls on all fours, stands again. I can't keep up and I lose sight of him when the gallery curves to the left. It's only twenty seconds but I'm relieved when it straightens out and I can see him again. We've reached a larger gallery, with rails on the floor, and we can stand upright.

'You're in good shape!'

He laughs.

'Yeah, I'm still pretty fit. My comrades, if they're not dead they've got miner's disease, silicosis. Lots of them are bedridden. My neighbour, he can't take four steps without the oxygen bottle. He walks from his bed to the door, from the door to his bed. I'm good, thank God.'

He points to a narrow shaft, silted up with rocks: a chimney.

'That's from the Spaniards, from the colonial times. They used stone hammers, we still find them sometimes. In this part of the mine there are chimneys like this one, full of rocks they threw away because all they wanted was silver. They chucked them down from the levels above, the chimneys gradually filled up. The ore wasn't pure enough for the Spaniards, but it's plenty pure for us. Plenty. When Comibol was here, emptying the chimneys was forbidden, they said the mountain would collapse.' (Comibol is the Bolivian state mining company.) 'Now, everyone does what they want. Some gangs empty the chimneys. Others mine the columns the Spaniards left in the chambers. You can't touch the columns, the roof falls in. But the ore in the columns is very pure, the miners dig out the rock, they dig it out and dig it out, while it holds. Until one day it doesn't.'

Villca's cheeks are the colour of copper, the skin smooth and taut, but his eyes are framed by deep lines, as if forty years working underground had carved his face into a mask. When he tells some terrible story he smiles as if slightly embarrassed and his eyes are submerged in creases: small eyes, red as embers, full of life.

His son, Federico, started in the mine when he was thirteen. One day he was helping a driller who was working at the face when the ground gave way under their feet. They only fell a few metres, dragged down by an avalanche of rocks, and they managed to scramble back up to the gallery. The driller and Federico ran for it. They were still running when a huge crash shook the mountain and a blast of dust knocked them headlong. Behind them, the whole gallery had caved in. The kid came out covered in blood and dust. He didn't want to go back into the mine. He found work on a building site, carrying loads of bricks and sacks of cement. In the open air.

I follow Villca along the large gallery, which I think is finally leading back to the outside, back to a different opening from the one we entered two hours ago, but I have no way of knowing. Although I say 'large gallery', it's only two and a half metres high and three metres wide. In the darkness, we splash through long, deep puddles, our lamps spilling stains of yellow light on the walls.

Villca says, 'This is a stroll in the park.'

And he stops.

We listen to the dripping, the subterranean sounds, the whispering of the rocks.

Villca turns slowly, sweeps the darkness with his helmet lamp and suddenly illuminates a human form, a man sitting against the wall, his eyes staring and a demented grin on his face. It's the devil. A devil sculpted in clay, with twisted horns, a wide mouth that stretches from ear to ear, and a dozen cigarette butts between his lips. Villca walks over to him, smiling, lights another cigarette and delicately places it in the devil's mouth.

'There you go, Tío.'

The Tío is the spirit that rules the depths, the patron of the miners, the one that fertilizes Pachamama, mother earth, to produce the seams of ore. If he's content, he makes the seams appear; if he's angry, he causes rockfalls. In the Tío's lap lie boxes of cigarettes, bottles of rough liquor, and a tangle of streamers, confetti and coca leaves that the miners throw during the *challas*, the thanksgiving ceremonies. He smiles and sits with his legs wide open, showing off his principal attribute: a huge, erect penis.

Villca unscrews a half-litre bottle of Guabirá, the 96° proof liquor that the miners drink during their breaks, neat or diluted with a little water and sugar. He holds the bottle to the Tío's mouth and pours its contents down the statue's throat. The alcohol bubbles out of the tip of the penis. Villca chuckles.

'One day we had a visit from María Álvarez, the vice-minister for mining. We let her come in but we said: Madam, you've got to kiss the tip of his member. If a woman wants to enter the mine, first she has to kiss the tip of the Tío's member. She bent down and she gave him a kiss right there.'

Villca laughs and walks on. At the diagonal intersection with another gallery, we hear voices. Villca sticks his head round the corner and shouts:

'Sons of bitches!'

* * *

When I come out I want to kiss the light, gulp it down, smear it all over my face.

My shadow moves along the slope. It climbs the rocks, stretching and shrinking as it advances, feeling its way across the mountainside. Cerro Rico was a majestic red pyramid when I saw it from afar two days ago; the mountain I am walking on today is a pile of rubble. It crunches beneath my feet, as if the loose stones could slip at any moment, dragging others in their wake; isolated rockpiles at first and then the whole mountainside sliding 800 metres in an avalanche that would bury the huts of the guards, then the miners' districts, and on down to the squares, the streets, the grand colonial houses, the baroque palaces, so that only the twin towers of the cathedral would be visible poking up through a sea of stone.

After 500 years of mining, Cerro Rico is crumbling. Every day, the miners remove three or four thousand tons of rock to obtain silver, lead, zinc and tin. According to the calculations of Osvaldo Arce, a geologist, the mountain still contains 47,824 tons of pure silver: more than have been removed in its entire history. The problem is that the silver is no longer concentrated in rich seams. Instead, it is to be found in tiny veins, at very low concentrations. The only way to get all the metal out would be to extract, crush and process the entire mountain.

That's what they seem to be doing: 8,000, 10,000, 12,000 miners go underground every day and carry on drilling. They work for thirty-nine cooperatives. On the outside, a big mining company – Manquiri, owned by a US multinational – processes their output. It also processes the *pallacos*, the huge deposits of rock and gravel that the miners extracted for centuries and discarded because the proportion of ore was too low. With modern technology, it's profitable for the company to crush these mountains of rubble and extract the silver and zinc from them.

Every dynamite explosion opens another hole in the Cerro. A study by the Ministry for Mines identified 138 rockfalls – some of them recent, others centuries old – and it also identified many points in the labyrinth of galleries where the risk of collapse is particularly acute. There are huge caverns, abandoned by the miners, which are crumbling as the acidic waters eat away at them. In 2011, after heavy rainfall, the pointed peak of the mountain began to disintegrate and in just a few days a crater 40 metres wide and 40 metres deep had opened up. The mountain is 4,800 metres tall; the government prohibited all mining operations above an altitude of 4,400 metres, the zone that is weakest.

The mountain of Cerro Rico is, among other things, a symbol. It's the great pyramid that looms over the city of Potosí, the silhouette that appears on Bolivia's coat of arms and on the country's stamps, on posters and postcards, in baroque landscape paintings; it's a huge triangular monument, an icon of earthly wealth and of divine power. But it's collapsing. In Bolivia's newspapers, columnists write of their fear that the nation's symbol could be mutilated. Or that it could crumble. The metaphors abound.

Meanwhile, unconcerned by the future of the coat of arms, thousands of miners enter the mountain every day.

The inhabitants of Potosí fear the day of the final collapse, the apocalyptic avalanche that will bring the history of Cerro Rico to a close. Inside the mountain lie the bones, or the dust of the bones, of tens of thousands of miners, from the first Indian slave in the times of the Spanish colony down to Luis Characayo, the driller who was named in yesterday's paper after he was crushed by a rockfall. Cause of death: fractured skull, severe brain trauma and asphyxia. Cerro Rico has another name. *La montaña que devora hombres*. The mountain that eats men.

* * *

Alicia Quispe is fourteen years old. She is wearing tatty yellow overalls (the sleeves several inches too long) a pair of oversized rubber boots, and a miner's helmet over black hair which is tied back in a ponytail. Her almond eyes are constantly shifting, as if she is looking to see what's going on behind me.

* * *

I've been told she'll come out soon. It's seven o'clock in the morning: this is my second visit to Cerro Rico and I'm relieved I don't have to go inside the mountain again. I don't mind waiting here on the *canchamina*, the rough esplanade of blue-grey dust, 4,400 metres up, in front of one of the 569 entrances recorded in a recent report on Cerro Rico. There are two Toyota Corolla cars belonging to the miners, four empty trucks for transporting the ore – three of them so rusty they appear to have been abandoned – and a pile of rails to replace the ones inside the mine when they are eventually corroded by acid and worn down by the trucks. The esplanade is also home to two huts built of adobe bricks and covered with corrugated iron. One of them is a store where the miners keep their tools; the other is the house where Alicia lives.

I read the local newspaper, *El Potosí*. There was another accident yesterday:

TWO MINE WORKERS DIE IN
ROCKFALL INSIDE MINE

Two mine workers aged 37 and 41 have died after being buried by a rockfall inside the Encinas mine, Cerro Rico, Potosí, according to public prosecutor, Fidel Castro. The tragic accident occurred as both men were extracting ore, a preliminary investigation has found. 'Unfortunately, due to an occupational accident, both men have died, one with a closed thoracic trauma and the other with a closed cranioencephalic trauma. They appear to have been buried by a rockfall in the mine,' the public prosecutor stated.

The bodies were removed by a state forensic team and personnel from the Special Anti-Crime Force.

The families of the miners have collected the bodies for burial.

I come across an item like this every few days: miners crushed by rockslides or who fall down shafts. Occasionally, one is killed by a dynamite explosion or falls into the grinding machine. Dozens die every year: you have to trawl through scattered sources of information; there are no clear comprehensive statistics. There are other kinds of information that don't generally appear in the newspapers or on the news or in the official documents, information that goes unreported. Of silicosis, there is the odd mention. Of violence, not even a whisper.

The mountain trembles. Softly at first, a vibration that is scarcely perceptible. Then the sound of metal and rock gradually grows from a rumble to a deafening thunder. A truck appears at the entrance to the mine, loaded with stones, and rolls past me at full speed. Pushing it are two miners wearing overalls, helmets and boots, one tall, the other short, their arms held straight as they strain against the truck, their heads tucked between their shoulders, their legs taking short rapid steps. They continue for another fifty metres, until the rails run out, at the edge of an embankment. A third miner is waiting for them. He walks over to the truck, stands on the lever that releases the hopper, and tips its contents out onto the slope. Two or three times a week, a lorry comes to remove the accumulated rocks.

The two adult miners – one of the miners who was pushing the truck and the one waiting on the esplanade – rub their blue hands on their overalls, take cigarettes from their inside pockets, and light them. It's quarter past seven in the morning and their shift is over.

The third miner, the shorter of the two pushing the truck, is a girl: Alicia Quispe, fourteen years old, wearing oversized clothes. One of the adults offers her a bottle of water and she takes a long swig.

I don't approach, I stay fifty metres away, wandering back and forth across the esplanade. I hope they'll take me for a tourist, even though it's a bit early. I'm carrying a backpack and a compact camera, and I take some photos –

of the mountain, of the entrance to the mine – and when I turn towards them I nod in greeting. Alicia sees me, recognizes me, but doesn't respond. I walk slowly away from the mine towards her house.

Alicia Quispe is not her real name. I prefer to conceal it so that she isn't dismissed from her clandestine employment. From the job that a director of the mining cooperatives will tell me doesn't exist. That doesn't exist but which, well, if it did exist wouldn't be such a big deal, because the kids, you know, they already live here, at the mine entrance, they help their families, like we used to, they say at the cooperative, like we've always done, because what would they do otherwise, the children of Cerro Rico?

Alicia performs a job that doesn't exist, a job that used to pay her twenty pesos a day – or rather, twenty pesos a night – a bit more than two dollars. And which now doesn't pay her anything at all. Now she works for free to pay off a debt that the miners in the cooperative attribute to her mother, a trap to keep them enslaved.

Yesterday I spoke to Alicia in a classroom at the foot of the mountain, where Cepromin organizes special lessons for the children of the mines (and other working children: construction workers, domestic servants, shoeshine kids) to keep them from falling behind with their schoolwork. And where they also eat eggs, meat and fresh vegetables – all the things they never get at home. Where they can have a hot shower and spend time playing, reading, relaxing. Where nobody hits them. The teachers told me I had to meet her. The first time I saw her she was sitting at a long table, with four or five other girls of her age, all doing their homework; she was leafing through an illustrated edition of *Cinderella*. I went over to say hello, talked to them, asked them some clumsy questions, and Alicia was the only one who asked me a question in return. I carried on speaking to her while her friends went back to their homework, and she invited me to come and visit her at home if I wanted to.

* * *

Cepromin is the Centro de Promoción Minera, an association founded in 1979 when the military dictatorship was in its death throes and Bolivian democracy was just beginning to emerge. The mining unions had been one of the most powerful forces in the struggle for freedom. And at the start of the 1980s they were full of enthusiasm.

'The miners had spent many years fighting to overthrow the dictatorship, and now it was time to take part in democracy. Cepromin was created to provide miners with political training, to prepare leaders, with the idea that the profits of the mining industry should no longer be sent abroad but should instead, for the first time in our history, serve the interests of the country.' I was listening to the organization's director, Cecilia Molina, in her office in La Paz. 'And look at us now. It's all gone. We just work to survive. Look at our projects: food programmes, schemes to combat extreme poverty, campaigns against child labour. Thirty years ago there were no children in the mines. Things happen for a reason; the poverty is the result of political decisions. In 1985 the state abandoned all but one of the mines, it dismissed 23,000 miners, privatized everything and allowed the law of the jungle to prevail. Now, the exploitation is shocking. There are thousands of miners working without contracts, without medical insurance, without pension contributions, earning a pittance, often being cheated because they're illiterate, and at the same time businesses are getting rich. The biggest problem is ignorance: there's no training, no awareness, no resistance. Every miner does what he can to earn a bit of cash and that's it. Then they have an accident or get silicosis and they're plunged into poverty, them and their families. The mines are much more dangerous than they used to be, because there's no technology and no safety measures. We just pray to the Tío and hope for the best. If a father dies at the age of thirty or thirty-five then his kids have to go down the mine.'

The Bolivian government calculated that there were 3,800 children working in the mines in 2011. Cepromin puts the figure at 13,000.

'It's impossible to give a precise number,' Molina says, 'because they're clandestine workers, and the figure goes up and down depending on mineral prices. The only thing you can be sure of is that if they start working at the age of twelve or fourteen then they won't make it to thirty-five.'

* * *

Alicia says goodbye to the two miners and walks the short distance to the hut where she lives with her mother Rosa (aged forty-two) and her sister Evelyn (aged four). It's not much more than a cubicle of rough adobe bricks, four walls with no windows and a metal roof. The miners built it here on the *canchamina*, 4,400 metres up, where it is lashed by the wind. The roof is held down by rocks to stop it from blowing away. Up here – whipping up clouds of toxic dust and showers of gravel that spatter like hailstones – the wind takes no prisoners.

The miners gave Alicia and her family permission to live here. It's the only place where they can live: a place where life is almost impossible.

Theirs is one of the highest houses on the planet, in the last and thinnest layer of human habitation, at an altitude of more than 4,400 metres, where they are almost alone. Alicia, Rosa and Evelyn have 99.9 per cent of humanity below them. Only a little higher up, all possibility of permanent life ends. The atmosphere thins out, the air has only half the density it has at sea level, and the lobes of the human lung struggle to pass sufficient quantities of oxygen into the bloodstream. The populations that live at these altitudes have adapted over the millennia: their lungs are larger so they can absorb more air at each breath, and they have more red blood cells to transport oxygen around their bodies. But there's a limit to the concentration of red blood cells, otherwise the blood becomes too thick, causing it to clot and giving rise to strokes and heart attacks. No human being can live permanently above 5,500 metres.

Here, at 4,400 metres, not everyone can take the strain. Almost all the recent arrivals suffer from headaches: we get dizzy, we become frightened when we realize how fast our hearts are beating. We take a few days to acclimatize, we sleep, rest, drink infusions of coca leaves, and wait for our red blood cells to multiply so that we can finally take a few steps without becoming exhausted. Some find it a bit harder: they vomit, they faint, they get migraines. Or a lot harder: fluid accumulates in their lungs or their brains, and they die.

Alicia is allowed to live here, where life is almost impossible.

The hut looks out over the *altiplano*, the Andean high plateau, a plain of ochre and salt that shimmers under the sun, dissolving into an aspirin-coloured sky. Not a single tree grows up here. Everything is stone and light. Here and there a hill bulges out, but it is as if the world is tired by the time it makes it to this height, and that's why the eruption of Cerro Rico is so impressive: a peak that stands 1,000 metres above the exhausted *altiplano*. The city of Potosí spreads out at the foot of the mountain, 200,000 inhabitants, with its neighbourhoods of little square houses and flat roofs, a network of closely packed cells, as if the city's geometry was the work of insects. Or a camp, housing pioneers who have come to extract the wealth from an uninhabitable planet.

That's exactly what it is. Alicia lives on the mountain of solid silver that dazzled the Spanish *conquistadores*: the divine gift that was the reward for their efforts, laying the foundations for their empire and confirming their beliefs. The Quechua word for this place was adopted by the Spanish as a synonym of unimaginable wealth: a *potosí*.

Alicia lives in Potosí, in the land of fabulous treasures.

This time she greets me and she invites me into the hut. The door is a sheet of metal with a small padlock; from the lintel hang blue and green strips, and two red plastic flowers. It's dark inside, the floor is beaten earth, and my eyes need time to become accustomed to the lack of light before they can make out more details. Little by little I see that the walls of the brick house, a cube measuring six metres by three, are covered inside with a layer of crumbling plaster. And I can hear the wind whistling through the cracks. Some of the cracks are covered with posters. Disney's Little Mermaid sits smiling on a rock at the bottom of the sea, next to a yellow fish, which is also smiling, and a red crab with bulging eyes, waving its happy claws. Beneath the seabed of the Disney poster a damp patch makes its way down the wall, turning the floor to mud. In the dim light I make out a gas ring on a table, a bed with thick blankets where the mother and the two girls sleep, half a dozen canvas sacks that serve as wardrobes, three old plastic chairs and another table where they eat and where Alicia usually does her homework.

Alicia opens her fist and shows me three stones the colour of lead, speckled with sparkling spots: particles of silver. She has pilfered them from the mine.

She wraps the stones in newspaper, puts the package in her backpack and disappears behind the canvas sacks to change her clothes. She takes off the overalls and puts on some jeans, a blue tracksuit top and a knitted hat. She grabs the backpack, and we leave the hut and walk downhill.

She's fourteen years old, and her hands are dry and tough, bleached by the dust of the mountain.

The wind sweeps the slopes: fragments of rock scatter before it, the rubble groans. The dust of Cerro Rico gets in your eyes, between your teeth, into your lungs. It contains arsenic, which causes cancer, and it contains cadmium, zinc, chrome and lead, all of which accumulate in the blood, gradually poisoning the body until it is exhausted. The dust also contains silver: between 120 and 150 grams of silver for every ton of dust. Every visitor takes away a few particles of Potosí silver in their lungs. It's because of these particles, the need to separate them from all the others, that Alicia lives in an adobe hut on the mountain.

'I used to go to Pailaviri to sell the stones. The tourists buy them there. Lots. But the kids in Pailaviri chased me away, because they sell stones too. Now I go down to the main square.'

'Do people buy them in the square?'

'Yes. But I have to watch out for the police.'

We hear a distant explosion, from underground. Grey dust rises from the mountain again, high into the air; it falls slowly, coming to rest on people and on the slope, then the lorries stir it up again.

We go down to the miners' district, bare roads gradually giving way to asphalted streets with pavements, continuing for two kilometres until we reach the main square, Plaza 10 de Noviembre, which has gardens, fountains and benches. It's the old pleasure garden, the colonial heart of Potosí. Looking south from the square, above the churches and palaces, you can see the impressive pyramid of Cerro Rico. Standing on high pedestals, silhouetted against the mountain, are two female statues: Justice with her scales and Liberty holding the torch of freedom. At the feet of Justice and Liberty, on a bench, Alicia takes a wooden box from her backpack. It is divided into a grid of nine cells. She unwraps the silver-bearing rocks she found today and a few more from other days, and places them in the cells.

In Pailaviri – which has been exploited continuously since the sixteenth century – she sold her rocks to foreigners being taken on guided visits to the galleries. Now, she comes to the square and sets up at the corner of Calle Ayacucho and Calle Quijarro. Tourists on their way to visit the Mint go past. She shows them the open box with the stones on display.

'Madam. Buy silver ore. Silver from Potosí, madam.' She asks for five pesos, ten pesos.

A young tourist gives her twenty pesos for one of the stones. It's as much as she used to earn in a whole night pushing trucks in the mine, before they made her work for nothing. Sometimes, Alicia tells me, a tourist gives her as much as fifty pesos for a stone. But the tourist guides and the police often chase the kids out of the square. She's always looking around her.

* * *

A hundred and fifty metres from the square, the National Mint is housed in a baroque fortress with massive walls, five courtyards and 200 rooms, with carved stone, cedar ceilings, and wrought iron from the Basque Country. The Mint still has the old Spanish machinery: furnaces to smelt the silver that was extracted from Cerro Rico; moulds to shape the liquid silver into ingots; rolling mills manufactured in Cadiz, the components brought by ship to Buenos Aires and carried overland by mule – four tons of iron and four tons of wood – all the way to Potosí. In one of the cellars, visitors can see the giant wheels that were turned by mules and powered the mills on the floor above.

Animals were not the only source of power. The forges and the machinery were also driven by Indians, urged on by overseers with whips who sometimes locked their charges in the dungeons. The best artisans in the empire were employed to perform the skilled work: assayers, forgemasters, cutters, diemasters, engravers. At the beginning of the colonial period, Potosí produced *macuquinas*, irregular coins that were hammered out by hand. But the rolling mills produced perfect discs of silver, which were then minted to make ducats, maravedis, pesetas and pesos – Castilian pesos, assayed pesos, *pesos de cruz, pesos de tres cuartillos, pesos columnarios*.

In coins and ingots, on the backs of mules and aboard fleets of galleons, the Spaniards removed 35,578 tons of fine silver from Cerro Rico de Potosí between 1545 and 1825, according to the estimates of nineteenth-century Irish geographer Joseph Pentland. At today's prices, that is the equivalent of 17 billion dollars. Mining engineer and former government minister Jorge Espinoza points out that – over so many centuries – it is not such a vast amount of money, not enough to sustain Potosí's reputation for fabulous wealth. Yields were low, far lower than those of today's mining enterprises. The secret of Potosí was not silver. Or not just silver: it was slave labour, which meant that extraction costs were low and the profit margins were huge.

It was not silver that provided the wealth of Potosí. It was the Indians.

'The Indians were subject to the most extreme physical hardship, driven to bodily exhaustion, trapped in blind servitude,' wrote the Bolivian historian Gabriel René Moreno. 'They were beasts of burden, like the steam energy that is measured in horsepower. Work was measured in Indians: the size of a load was measured by how many Indians would be required to carry it, farmland by the number of Indians needed to plough it in a day. The

Indians were distributed in accordance with the law, or outside of the law, or against the law, nobody cared which, so long as they were implacably distributed.'

Inside the Mint, visitors can view *La Virgen del Cerro*, an eighteenth-century painting by an unknown artist, the most impressive piece in the entire collection. It shows a fusion of two worlds, the Inca and the Christian. The pyramid of Cerro Rico is transformed into the cloak of the Virgin Mary, who is presented as a mountain goddess, an earth mother, a Christianized Pachamama. A crown is being placed on her head by the Father, the Son and the Holy Ghost, escorted by the archangels Michael and Gabriel, on a celestial stage held aloft by clouds and cherubs. Beneath the clouds the coronation is witnessed by the Inca sun god Inti and the moon god Quilla. Across the folds of the Virgin's cloak – which are also the slopes of Cerro Rico – wander vicuña, guanaco and horses. The mountain is criss-crossed by a network of galleries that enclose allegorical scenes: the thunder that expelled the vassals of the Inca emperor, Huayna Capac, when they tried to sink a shaft into the hillside and then, in the time of the Spaniards, the chance discovery of silver by the Indian, Huallpa. At the feet of the Cerro, to the right, praying and giving thanks, are the Pope, a cardinal and a bishop; to the left are the Emperor Charles V, a knight of the Order of Santiago, and another nobleman who may be the person who commissioned the painting. In the middle, at the bottom of the mountain, is the globe.

The whole world, lying at the feet of Cerro Rico de Potosí.

* * *

After an hour in the square, Alicia has sold two stones and has thirty pesos in her pocket. She walks towards Calle Nogales and raises her hand to hail a shared taxi. For two pesos it will take her to the miners' district, at the top of the city, and from there she will walk.

She once visited the Mint with her classmates. She saw the huge wheels and the cogs, the furnaces, the rooms of paintings from the period of the Spanish viceroyalty, the altarpieces, the velvet-upholstered chairs, the tables inlaid with mother-of-pearl, the picture frames gilded with gold leaf, the coin collection, the rooms full of silverware: silver tables, silver chalices, silver tureens, silver vases, silver statues, silver suits of armour. But it was something else that made the biggest impression.

'The children.'

In the archaeology room, several mummified children are displayed in glass cases. Some of them are indigenous, from the twelfth and fourteenth centuries, just skin and bone. Others, smaller, some mere babies, are the children of Spanish colonists, in hats, lace finery and slippers.

* * *

The powerful Inca ruler Huayna Capac, eleventh king of Cusco and third emperor of Tawantinsuyu, possessed heaps of gold and piles of silver. In the royal palace, gold statues commemorated his predecessors; golden trees, flowers and grass adorned the gardens; even the quern stones used to grind the maize in the palace kitchens were fashioned from gold.

After defeating the Guaraní armies which had devastated his Peruvian provinces, and massacring 6,000 of their soldiers, he was received at Cantumarca with great celebrations. There he saw Sumac Orcko – the beautiful mountain – and, amazed by its size and beauty, he declared to his courtiers, 'Within this mountain lies much silver.'

Huayna Capac ordered his vassals to dig into the beautiful mountain and extract the valuable metal. They brought tools of hardwood and flint, climbed the slopes, and located the seams. But no sooner had they begun to work than a blast of thunder shook the mountain. A harsh voice split the sky and roared, 'Do not take the silver from this mountain! It belongs to other masters.' The terrified workers ran to the king to tell him they had heard a 'great roar' (*potocsi* in their language) and so the mountain became known as Potosí.

Huayna Capac prophesied that, after his death, the realm would be invaded by strangers from a distant land, who would seize the empire from his sons, overthrowing their rule and destroying their idols.

According to the chronicler Bartolomé Arzáns de Orsúa y Vela, these events occurred eighty-three years before the Spaniards discovered the famous mountain.

'At that time,' wrote Arzáns,

the Indians extracted valuable metals from the hills because they knew the secrets of the mountain and where the ore was to be found. But when they saw the avarice and barbarity of the Spaniards they closed up the mine shafts and threw everything they had extracted from the mountain into the deep lake of Chucuito or buried it wherever they were when the news reached them. Such, however, was the Spaniards' hunger for gold and silver that, not satisfied with their finds, they forced the unfortunate Indians, without pity or mercy, to reveal the whereabouts of their riches, and with great violence compelled them to bring forth the precious metals.

Many of the Indians, unable to withstand such brutality, fled to the far corners of Peru to live among strangers. Some took their own lives. Others gathered together in bands of fifty or a hundred, with their wives and children, in the caves and gorges of the mountains, where they starved to death. Yet others fell into the hands of the Spaniards and were taken as slaves, unprotected by reason, law or charity.

One may thus say that those Spaniards reduced Peru to tyranny. Millions of Indians and vast quantities of gold and silver were consumed, and Peru became a shadow of what it had been in the time of its kings.

Temporal riches were destroyed, replaced by the heavenly riches of the one true God, whom the Indians were now able to adore.

Some say that Diego Huallpa was a llama herder on the slopes of Potosí, and one night he was looking for a lost animal when darkness fell, so he lit a fire and lay down to sleep. Others say he was a mining expert, sent by the new Spanish governors to prospect for ore, when he slipped and grasped a quinoa bush to save himself from falling, ripping the plant out by the roots. In the first version of the story, he spotted a glimmer of silver in the embers of the fire. In the second version, flecks of the precious metal sparkled in the roots of the bush.

On 1 April 1545, Captain Juan de Villarroel, on behalf of the Spanish crown, took possession of the mountain,

the famous, magnificent, rich and inexhaustible Cerro Rico de Potosí. Singular work of the power of God, unique miracle of nature, most perfect and permanent marvel of the world. Delight of mortals, emperor of mountains, king of hills, prince of minerals, lord of five thousand Indians who bring forth its entrails. Bugle that sounds across the globe, mercenary army fighting the enemies of the faith, fortress and bulwark that thwarts their designs, cannon whose shot destroys them. Enticer of men, magnet of their desires, foundation of all treasures, ornament of sacred temples, coin with which heaven is purchased. Monster of wealth, body of earth, soul of silver, whose fifteen hundred mouths cry out to humans so it may give them its treasures. Known in every corner of the world, the property of Catholic sovereigns, the envy of other monarchs. That which nations admire, whose power they acclaim, whose excellence they approve. Sublime without equal, celebrated as admirable, praised as most perfect. Provider of untarnished silver, which men defy the wind to acquire, cross the seas to find, disturb the earth to possess.

The slaves who had been brought from Angola were unable to withstand the cold or the altitude sickness, and died of exhaustion after extracting a few hundredweight of rock.

And so the viceroy, Francisco de Toledo, created the *mita*, a system of forced Indian labour. The Spaniards initially calculated that the mines of Potosí would require 4,500 forced labourers a year but the workers died so quickly that the Spaniards organized them into three gangs, with each group working for one week followed by two weeks of rest. This measure meant that 13,500 Indians were required each year, recruited exclusively from the high plateau so that they would be unaffected by altitude sickness. The levy lasted for one year, after which the labourers were free for the next six. In theory, this meant that 94,500 Indians were rotated in seven-year cycles, but the terrible death rates in the mines meant that far higher numbers had to be recruited.

Some of the labourers were brought to Potosí from many hundreds of miles away. Spanish soldiers entered the villages and rounded up the men. They also took the llamas, loaded with sacks of potatoes and maize, as provisions for the journey. And they took the wives and children of the labourers, too, as hostages to prevent the men from fleeing. During the forced march across the plateau, children died and pregnant women miscarried or gave birth to infants who survived for a few hours at most.

Upon arrival, the terrified labourers descended into the mines of Potosí. They were forced to crawl through tunnels and prise away the rock with iron crowbars. When there weren't enough crowbars, they scraped at the rock face with cows' horns or with their naked hands. They spent a whole week below ground, snatching a few hours' sleep, eating stale bread and chewing on coca leaves. The plant had been condemned in 1551 by the First Ecclesiastical Council of Lima for its diabolical properties and because it was seen as a barrier to Christianity, but it was soon rehabilitated when the authorities found that its stimulant effect enabled the forced labourers to work for two whole days without eating.

Despite this, the Indians were not productive enough for their overseers. Judge Juan de Matienzo, a future governor of Potosí, sent a report to Philip II in 1567.

The Indians are cowardly, weak and stubborn. They immediately and without cause succumb to anxiety and anger, but if you ask them why, they are unable to answer. As a result, they become desperate and hang themselves, young and old alike, at any time and at the slightest mishap or fright. They are given to drinking and idolatry, and when in their cups commit the most serious of crimes. They are generally depraved. They have been born to serve and to learn manual trades, at which they are skilled. They are very slow and do not like to be hurried. They are enemies of toil and friends of idleness, unless they be forced to work.

By 1600, the miners had already reached a depth of 700 metres, and took five hours to reach the surface, hauling sacks of ore weighing thirty or forty kilos or enormous skins full of the toxic water that had to be bailed out of the galleries.

* * *

'Pickaxe blows echo through the rich yet terrifying entrails of this wondrous mountain,' wrote Arzáns,

> mingling with the voices of some, the groans of others, the shouts of the Spanish foremen, the chaos and intolerable labour of all, the terrifying thunder of gunpowder, a noise like that of hell itself. Countless souls perish there. Some are swallowed by the very

earth on which they tread, unaware of the cavities beneath, which open up and bury them alive. Others are entombed by loose rocks falling from above, or plunge into deep shafts and pools and are drowned. You will see Indians climbing the ropes loaded with ore, drenched in sweat, or descending narrow ladders to a depth of 200 or 300 yards or more, and often they lose their footing and plunge to their deaths. You will also see them walk like beasts on all fours, with burdens on their backs, or crawling on their bellies like worms.

When they emerged from beneath the ground, the workers had to carry the ore down the slope to the mills, where it was crushed, take the most promising pieces to the thousands of furnaces that burned at the mine entrances, and separate out the silver from the impurities. After a few decades, the veins of pure silver, white silver, ruby silver and rough lead were exhausted, and it became necessary to exploit the slag, the workings, and the poor-quality rock. Mercury or quicksilver was imported in leather skins from Almadén in Spain, where it was mined. At Potosí it was combined with the crushed rock in great vats, and mixed by the Indians with their bare legs to separate the ore from the stone.

The mercury slowly poisoned the workers. Their skin began to sting, their arms and legs became numb, their gums bled, they saw double or went blind, suffered coughing fits, were unable to breathe, shook all over, and died. When the owners of the mills noticed these effects, they became concerned that their mules might drink water that had been contaminated by mercury, and die. They decided to tether the mules farther away. A mule was much more valuable than an Indian.

* * *

In 1968, a priest called Marcelo told the writer Cees Nooteboom about a pig-borne disease that had spread through a Bolivian mining camp. The pigs had to be killed, otherwise people would fall ill. But the miners hid their pigs. 'We told them, "If you don't bring out your pigs, your children will die." But they stood firm in front of the bed beneath which they had hidden their pigs, and replied: "We can make children whenever we want, but who knows when we will have enough money to buy another pig?"'

* * *

The devout viceroy Pedro Fernández de Castro wrote to Charles II from Lima in 1670 to complain about the brutality visited upon the Indians in the mines of Potosí and Huancavelica. Because such excesses occurred under his rule, the viceroy was worried that the salvation of his soul was at peril.

* * *

Potosí was the navel of the world. A never-ending mule train connected it to the port of Arica on the Pacific coast, bearing silver bars for shipment to Spain, where they were squandered on luxuries, debt or war, and traded across the seven seas and the four continents. The mules returned from the coast to the mountain, loaded with the finest merchandise drawn from across the globe by the wealth and avarice of Potosí, transported in fleets of galleons escorted by the imperial navy from Sanlúcar de Barrameda in Spain to Portobello on the Caribbean, carried across the isthmus of Panama, and then shipped down the coast to the ports of Callao and Arica.

* * *

'Potosí reaps the harvest of silver,' wrote Arzáns,

and so can take its pick of the offerings of the world. And for the enjoyment of this precious metal, men walk and sail with their goods, ferrying them across unknown and disparate seas, climes and provinces, filling ships beyond number, which bring them over the Southern Sea, the Atlantic, the Mediterranean, the Adriatic, the Ionian, the Persian, the Black, the Indian, the Caspian and all the other seas of the world, and every kingdom, province and city forgoes sleep so that it may perfect the most novel products that they may serve and please Potosí.

From beloved Spain each province sends that in which it outdoes its rivals. Taffeta, silk and other textiles from Granada, Priego and Jaén. Woollens and swords from Toledo. Satin and silk from Valencia and Murcia. Decorated fans, wooden cases and a thousand playthings and curiosities from Madrid. Iron from Biscay. The richest thread from Portugal. Textiles, white lace, gold- and silverware, worsted cloth, beaverskin hats and all manner of fine linen from France. Canvases and cloths from Holland. Swords, steel and table linen from Germany. Paper from Genoa. Silk from Calabria and Puglia. Stockings and textiles from Naples. Bombazine and satin from Florence. Beautiful embroidered cloths and the finest textiles from Tuscany. Elegant gold and silver lace, and rich fabrics from Milan. Exquisite paintings and engravings from Rome. Cloths, hats and every kind of woollen cloth from England. The clearest crystal from Venice. Beeswax from Cyprus, Candia and the coasts of Africa. Cochineal, glass, tortoiseshell, ivory and precious gems from India. Diamonds from Ceylon, perfumes from Arabia, and carpets from Persia, Cairo and Turkey. Every kind of spice, musk and civet from Terranate, Molucca and Goa. White porcelain and silken garments from China. Negroes from Cape Verde and Angola. Cochineal, indigo, vanilla, cocoa and the finest wood from New Spain. Timber from Brazil. Pepper and spices from the Moluccas. Pearls for which they dive in the East Indies, the Island of Margarita, Panama, Cubagua, Puerto Viejo and other places. Gemstones and mother of pearl, bracelets and necklaces, headdresses and broaches. Rich cloths, hessian, cambric, linen, cotton canvas, canopies, carpets, hats and other textiles from Quito, Riobamba, Otavalo, Latacunga, Cajamarca, Tarama, Bombón, Guamalíes, Huánuco, Cuzco and other provinces of the Spanish Indies. Accomplished portraits and pictures wrought with great skill upon fine canvases from Chachapoyas. And wax, elk skins, battens, soft leather, bees' honey, cotton fibres and cloth, baskets and resins from Tucumán, Santa Cruz de la Sierra, Misque, Cochabamba and other provinces and cities.

In addition to all these things, in this city one can find, brought here from all parts of the world, the most precious stones, diamond, emerald, pantaura, ruby, jacinth, topaz, turquoise, sapphire, amethyst, chalcedony, pink rubies, garnets, aventurine, girasol, candite, and an abundance of lodestones, agate, jade, coral, jasper and other bright stones of less renown.

In Alicia's hut, there are two plastic jerrycans manufactured in China. They are used to collect and store water.

* * *

It's Sunday. Alicia didn't work last night and she's having a quiet morning, sitting at the table doing her homework. She has to plan the outline for a radio programme containing local news items, interviews and music. She writes in a large exercise book with a picture of an American basketball player on the cover and pages marked out with gridlines. She draws three columns, headed 'topic', 'audio resource' and 'time'.

'I like going to school, but sometimes it's hard because I'm tired.'

In the first column, she jots down a list of news items: miners go on strike against taxes, bus accident with four dead, football match between Real Potosí and Nacional Potosí. In the second column, she writes two items: *La ciudad que habita en mí* ('The city that lives in me', a song by Bolivian rock band Octavia); and an interview with the chairman of the residents' association of the mining district of La Concepción. Then she writes her questions. Why did you become chairman? What are the biggest problems in the neighbourhood? Do the residents help you?

When Alicia is nearly finished, her mother tells her it's time to go and fetch water. Rosa Quispe carries an invisible load. She is short, hunched over, still strong enough to work but with the slow movements and permanent grimace of a woman who is nearing old age. I have to remind myself that she is only forty-two. She wears a blue woollen coat and a very dusty, wide-brimmed, black hat which hides her eyes.

Alicia and Rosa take the two jerrycans and a plastic bottle with the top cut off. They walk 100 metres to a nearby gully. A stream trickles through it, the water gathering in brown pools that give off a sharp odour. The water comes from the mines, mixed with earth and minerals.

Rosa bends down, fills the bottle and empties it into the first can. She repeats the action several times until the can is full.

'It's not for drinking,' she explains. 'Just cooking.'

'But isn't it very dirty?'

'Yes. If anyone from the mining company sees us, they tell us off. The security guards come and tell us the water's bad. But what can I do? Sometimes I send the girls down to the Care Centre in town and they give us cans with clean water, but they're heavy and it's a long way. We can't always go up and down the mountain. The council should send a truck to deliver water. But we're not legal, so they don't come. It's like we don't exist.'

Mother and daughter walk back to the hut, each carrying a can weighing ten to fifteen kilos.

'We don't drink it. We use it for washing clothes and cooking. I just make noodle soup with it.'

'And how does it taste?'

'A bit strange. With stains floating on it, like oil.'

'Have you had stomach pains or been unwell?'

'Yes, all the time. Our tummies are never quite right, we get the runs. Then there's Alicia's kidney. I don't know if it's the water or the dust in the mine.'

She explains that Alicia's left kidney doesn't work. A year ago she was in a lot of pain and was taken to hospital.

'They gave her lots of jabs. Poor little Ali. She just lay there, her face was purple and her lips were all swollen. She didn't talk. Thank God she recovered.'

Alicia is silent, looking at the floor. She says she's okay.

'Now I take pills. They're to make my kidney better, so it starts working again. If it doesn't then I think they'll take it out. I know it's bad from working in the mine. My dad had kidney problems too.'

When they get back to the hut, Rosa and Alicia leave the cans in a corner, next to the gas ring they use for cooking. Alicia's four-year-old sister Evelyn is sitting on the bed, colouring in a comic with crayons. She is a miniature version of Alicia: the same long black hair, the same rosy cheeks, the same almond eyes, but with a playful expression, giggling and full of fun. I look at the faces of the two sisters – so similar and yet so different – the carefree laughter of the small girl, the serious, almost suspicious expression of the adolescent, and I realize just how grown up Alicia is at fourteen years of age.

Rosa shows me Evelyn's hands: they're covered with black warts.

'The first time they appeared, I cut them off with scissors. But they came back.'

The League for the Defence of the Environment analysed samples of dust in the towns around Cerro Rico de Potosí and found concentrations of heavy metals far higher than the limits established by the World Health Organization. It also tested blood samples from local people and found high levels of arsenic, cadmium, mercury, zinc and chrome. The air they breathe is loaded with heavy metals, the animals and vegetables they eat are full of heavy metals, the water they drink is saturated with heavy metals. They get warts on their skin and cysts on their eyes; their red blood cells are depleted; they suffer from anaemia, chronic fatigue, muscle pain, depression and hallucinations; their hair falls out and they develop tumours; their babies have neurological problems.

'It's ugly, living here,' says Rosa, sitting on the bed she shares with her two daughters. 'The *wawas*, the babies, have diarrhoea. The grown-ups have yellow teeth. The old people can't breathe. Our lungs dry out, you know? The dust gets inside and stays there, and your lungs dry out and go hard. That's how my husband died. That's how we're all going to die, gasping for breath.'

* * *

Potosí is the poorest department of the poorest country in South America. According to a study conducted in 2012 by the United Nations Population Fund, 94 per cent of its inhabitants are unable to satisfy their basic needs for a healthy diet, decent housing, drinking water, healthcare and education. And 46 per cent of the local population live in extreme poverty: they do not even earn enough money to keep them safe from starvation.

The people who live on the slopes of Cerro Rico are the poorest of the poor. In the barrios that cling to the sides of the mountain, three out of every four children suffer from chronic malnutrition: some die while others are stunted both physically and mentally. They eat one meal a day, a bowl of soup with noodles or rice and a few chunks of potato. They drink contaminated water. They inhale heavy metal dust. They sleep on mats on the floor covered by blankets, at an altitude of more than 4,000 metres.

Of every 1,000 children born on Cerro Rico, 188 will die before reaching the end of their first year, a rate that is five times higher than for Bolivia as a whole, ten times that of Latin America, and forty times that of Europe. Half of the inhabitants of Cerro Rico are illiterate. The life expectancy for women is forty-five and for men it is forty.

Around the turn of the millennium, rich deposits of silver, lead and zinc were discovered. At the same time, global ore prices rose steadily. In 2000, the mines of Potosí exported ore worth 188 million dollars; by 2008 the figure was 1,321 million dollars, and in 2011 it hit 2,456 million. The San Cristóbal mine, operated by a Japanese industrial group, extracted a daily yield of 1,300 tons of concentrated silver, zinc and lead from deposits on the south side of Potosí, from where they were despatched in sealed trains to the Chilean port of Mejillones for export to Asia, Australia and Europe. The mine was the world's third-largest producer of silver and the sixth-largest producer of zinc. In 2010 alone, it paid 147 million dollars in export duties, almost as much as all the other mines in the country combined.

Between 2004 and 2014, Bolivia experienced ten years of prosperity. The country exported gas and minerals, revenues grew, employment rose, wealth was redistributed and social policies were introduced to combat inequality and poverty (which fell from 63 to 39 per cent).

But Potosí did not enjoy the benefits.

Because the economy of Potosí is like a mining camp: raw materials are extracted and sent to other countries, and the wealth is extracted too. The large operations – the ones that generate most money – are mechanized and employ few workers. Most miners are members of small-scale artisan cooperatives. The few miners that prosper generally leave for Sucre to set up in business and buy a house, because the altitude is lower there, the climate is gentler, life is sweeter. Money leaves Potosí, the mining companies don't create much employment and the taxes they pay have not been used to diversify the local economy. There is no industry here to transform the ore, no jobs from subsidiary activities, no development, no investment. The government's scant levels of social spending – on health, sanitation, housing, education – are lower than what Potosí would qualify for on a purely per capita basis, even before one considers the higher levels of need in the poorest department in the country.

In 2010, during the mining boom, the government of Evo Morales announced a list of investments in Potosí: the construction of several hospitals, a hydroelectric power station, a cement factory, highways, an international airport. In 2013, ore prices began to fall. In July 2015, faced with strikes and protests in Potosí, the government said the airport and the cement factory were too expensive and that instead it would build a primary care hospital, upgrade the existing airport and continue to fill in the peak of Cerro Rico to stop it from collapsing.

* * *

'Alicia, what would you ask the government for?'

'To bring us water and electricity. Up here on the Cerro we have nothing.'

'And security too,' says Rosa. 'The miners rob us whenever they want. They steal tools from the cooperative and we get left with the debt.'

* * *

Today is Sunday and there's nobody in the mine, so Alicia takes me to the gallery where she works. It's easy: we leave the hut, walk twenty metres, put on a hard hat and follow the rails into the mountain. We pass through an entrance that is two metres high and a metre and a half wide, just big enough for the trucks.

We switch on the torches on our helmets. As soon as we enter the gallery we tread in puddles of orange mud. Alicia, who goes ahead, advises me to walk on the rails. I struggle to keep up because I'm clumsy, I have to think about every step I take, stooping so as not to bang my head on the roof. She turns from time to time, gives a faint smile and waits in silence.

We soon stop. She points at the wall but at first all I can see are some little plastic flags fixed to the rock and some coca leaves on the ground. Gradually, I make out an oval shape that has been cut into the wall, a crude face, with blind eyes and prominent lips. It's the Tío. A rudimentary Tío in a lesser gallery, because miners make offerings to the underground spirit at each entrance to the Cerro Rico.

'Do you pray to the Tío?'

'Sometimes I bring him some coca leaves and scatter them on the ground. Or I light a cigarette and give it to him.'

'And do you say anything to him?'

'Yes.'

'What do you say?'

'I don't know. I say, "Tío, I'm going in to work, help me, give me the ore, take care of me. Here's your coca. I need luck so that nothing happens to me, Tío, so the walls don't fall in."'

'A miner told me women shouldn't enter the mine. That the Tío falls in love with them and then Pachamama gets jealous and hides the ore.'

Alicia smiles, sceptically.

'Women aren't meant to go in. And the law says kids shouldn't, either.'

'And what do the miners in the cooperative think?'

'They don't mind, because I do as much work as them but they pay me less. A truck man gets 80 or 100 pesos a day, and I only get twenty for the same work. But they don't pay me now.'

She reaches out to pat the Tío and we walk on. Sometimes, Alicia explains, the truck gets stuck in the mud and the wheels come off the rails. When that happens she hangs onto one side of the truck and tries to rock it back into place. At other times, accidents are caused by trucks moving at high speed. The trucks are loaded with hundreds of kilos of rock and when the miners push them downhill, the trucks roll so quickly that they sometimes tip over when they reach a curve. If the truck man – or the truck girl – tries to slow the truck down, if they climb onto the truck or try to stop it, they run the risk of being squashed between the truck, the load and the wall.

Alicia points out a small side tunnel, a rabbit hole which opens up at ground level so that the only way to enter is by crawling and wriggling ...

'Like a lizard.'

... and this is one of those places where gas sometimes accumulates.

'There's a shaft near here where it comes and goes.'

'What?'

'Sometimes the shaft gives off gas, other times it doesn't. One time, two miners sat down to rest, to chew some coca leaves. And they fell asleep. The gas got them and they died. When the gas comes, it smells bad. Your head starts to feel strange, a bit heavy, you get dizzy, you can't see properly. If that happens, you have to take your boot off, quick. You take your boot off, put it on your face like this, covering your nose and mouth, breathe inside the boot and run for it.'

Alicia talks about the gas, the derailments and the other things she's afraid of: the rockfalls, the back pain that lasts for weeks at a time, the air loaded with dust that poisons her insides, has already paralysed one of her kidneys and which killed her father. Her dad died from silicosis when she was eight. He couldn't stop coughing, his face turned red, his whole body was fighting for air, each breath a terrifying whistle. He was suffocating. In the end, he died at home. She saw it. She talks, reluctantly, about the miners who drink a lot and who 'molest' girls. I ask her what she means. Two of her friends, aged fourteen and fifteen, were raped by miners and became pregnant.

She accepts all of these terrifying things because she is tormented by an even worse fear.

'Not long ago, a baby in Pailaviri died because the family had no food.'

Alicia has a four-year-old sister, her mother has debts, some weeks there is no money for rice, noodles or potatoes, so she has to go into the mine, push the trucks, breathe in the dust, watch out for the rockfalls.

The gallery is shored up with eucalyptus posts but the roof bulges like a donkey's stomach.

At the face, at the end of the gallery, piles of rocks lie scattered on the ground. Yesterday, the miners placed sticks of dynamite, lit the fuse and got away as fast as they could. The dynamite exploded, the rock face shattered and the dust gradually settled. Tomorrow, the miners will be back with empty trucks which they will load with shovel-fuls of rock. They will also hack at those parts of the wall where the rock has cracked but hasn't come away.

'This is the place that scares me the most. Sometimes there's just one rock holding up the whole face, but nobody knows and if you take that rock away, it all falls down.'

As we are walking back, Alicia tells me about a legend.

'People say nobody has ever reached the middle of the mountain, and that it's made of solid silver.'

'Do you believe them?'

'No way.'

*   *   *

Pearl is white, black and brown, a nervous young mongrel who scampers around the hut and barks whenever she sees a stranger. She picks up a scrawny black cat by the scruff of its neck, and carries it around in her jaws.

Alicia laughs.

'The cat's used to it. All our dogs have picked it up in their mouths like that.'

Alicia sits on an overturned truck next to the rails that come out of the mine. Today is Wednesday. She hasn't gone into the mine or gone down the mountain to sell stones in the square. She went to school in the morning and is spending the afternoon at home. She's wearing a Pink Panther tee-shirt, a brown tracksuit jacket with yellow sleeves, and her house key hangs from a string around her neck.

'Have you had a lot of dogs?'

'Yes, but they've all been poisoned. The thieves wait until we're out, then come and throw them poisoned meat.'

With Alicia are her mother, Rosa, and her aunt, Lorena. They sit on broken-down plastic chairs at the mine entrance and chew coca leaves. They put some leaves into their mouths, moisten them with saliva, form the wet leaves into a ball, and hold the ball inside their cheeks for hours.

Rosa and Lorena are both widows. When their husbands died, each was left with no income and a brood of children to look after. Lorena has seven and Rosa has four: Alicia, Evelyn, an older daughter who moved to Oruro in search of employment, and a son who migrated to Porco but came back to work in the mine and now lives in an apartment in town. Rosa and Lorena both had to leave their rented flats, accept the mining cooperative's offer and move up the mountain to live in an adobe hut next to the mine entrance. Up here they don't have water or electricity, it's cold and damp and the contaminated air makes them ill. But they don't have to pay any rent and they have a job: they're guards. They make sure nobody enters the mine and they look after the hut where the miners keep their drills, their tools, their boots and their clothes when they come off shift. In exchange, they receive the equivalent of forty dollars a month – less than half the minimum salary. They're also allowed to work as *palliris*, sweeping up the loose stones that fall off the trucks, gathering them up and breaking them into pieces with a hammer in search of a few grams of ore. The money they make from selling the ore helps them to subsist but when it's not enough – which is almost always – their adolescent children work in the mine to make some extra money.

Alicia was twelve when she first went into the mine. She was paid twenty pesos for pushing the trucks, a little over two dollars for a night working below ground.

She was paid.

Until one Sunday, when Rosa, Alicia and Evelyn went out for a couple of hours and disaster struck.

'Can't I even leave the hut for a couple of hours?' asks Rosa. She looks at the floor, her lips pressed tight, her brow furrowed. As she talks, she squeezes her hands and knots her fingers, which are swollen and twisted by arthritis.

That Sunday in December, she recalls, she went down to the Care Centre, a small building on the slopes of Cerro Rico, to attend a sewing course. She took her daughters with her because Care provides free meals for mining families on Sundays.

'I wasn't even away for two hours,' Rosa says. She starts to sob then holds it back. Her face sets in anger. 'Can't I even go out for two hours so my daughters can eat?'

After having lunch at the centre, Rosa stayed on for the second part of the course and sent the girls home with a can of clean water that had been donated to them.

Alicia and Evelyn scrambled back up the slope. When they reached the hut, they saw that someone had ripped the door off the store where the miners keep their tools. Alicia approached in terror, peered into the gloom and ran back down the hill.

'I remember her coming in,' says Rosa. 'She burst into the room, crying. She was very upset. "Mum, mum, they've stolen the tools!" The poor thing. We ran straight home. They'd taken three pneumatic drills. Seven hundred dollars each. And three new hand drills too. It makes me sad to think about it. I remember how much my daughters cried. And I saw them, and I cried even more. My God, who could have done this to us?'

The miners in the cooperative, as is usual in such cases, decided that Rosa had to reimburse them for the stolen materials: 2,000 dollars. What Rosa and her daughter would earn in two years. The cooperative withheld half of Rosa's salary and stopped paying Alicia for her night shifts until the debt had been repaid.

That's how Alicia started working in the mine for free and pilfering stones with traces of silver so she can sell them to tourists.

'We've all been robbed, every single one of us,' says Lorena. Alicia's aunt is fifty but, with sunken eyes and a large wart at the base of her nose, she looks closer to seventy. She has hoops in her ears, a red knitted hat covers messy white hair, and she has a black woollen shawl around her shoulders. 'Often the ones who steal are the *segundamanos.*'

'*Segundamanos?*'

'The labourers. They're called *segundamanos*, second-handers. The members of the cooperative use labourers who work at the rock face. The labourers don't have a contract or insurance or anything, sometimes they don't even get paid. Then they get angry and rob the cooperative members. They know where the tools are kept, they know that we guard them. When the miners go home, the labourers come and steal things. That's why we always have dogs, so they bark if someone comes in the night. If a thief comes we set off a stick of dynamite. It scares them off. Or we blow our whistles as loud as we can, so the other guards come running. We help each other. But sometimes we don't hear. The thieves come at night and throw a piece of meat to the dog. Always a nice chunk of meat. They put poison in it. They poison our dogs. We've all been robbed.'

Lorena is president of the guards' association in La Plata, one of the sectors of Cerro Rico. It's a small group, and almost all of the members are miners' widows.

'There are fifteen of us, and every single one of us has been robbed at least once. Some of us more. Three times, four times, five times. Then we have to work for nothing, to pay it back.'

Once, Lorena woke up at three in the morning to the sound of a nearby four-by-four. She came out of the hut to see two men removing the wheels and axles of a mine truck.

'Each wheel is worth 700 pesos,' she says. 'That time I was lucky, because another car with miners from the cooperative arrived. They'd seen the headlights and got suspicious. They came quickly, making noise and shouting at the thieves. The thieves ran away. The axles and the wheels are heavy, and the thieves just dumped them on the ground and escaped. Another night, we weren't so lucky. We didn't hear anything, we were all sleeping in the hut, my daughter Alexia, my grandson Roberto and me. Some men came and they took four wheels from a truck. We had to work for three months without pay. Alexia went to the mine to ask for work, to dig for ore, to earn a bit of money because otherwise we wouldn't have enough to eat.'

Alicia listens to her aunt. She seems uncomfortable, as if she would prefer not to have to listen to this story again.

'We always pay for things we haven't done,' Lorena continues. 'Our lives are sad. One sorrow ends and another one begins. Six years I've been living up on the Cerro and I can't get used to it. Up here, we're all sick. I get headaches because of my nerves, because I don't sleep properly. I'm always tired when I wake up.'

The litany of sorrows prompts more. Rosa touches the back of her neck.

'Last year I fell down. I banged my head on a rock. There was lots of blood. I had pain all the way up the back of my head, here. It still hurts. And it swells up. I guess it's from the fall but I don't know. When it hurts I get scared. I feel very tired, weak. And when they robbed us …'

She lets out a sigh when she remembers the robbery, the debt, the slave labour. She holds it in, breathes deeply and carries on talking.

'Sometimes I cry but never in front of the girls. Alicia already cries a lot. I feel desperate. I feel frozen inside, in my chest. Some days I feel better, I chew some coca leaves, I have energy, I sweep up the ore, break the stones, I think about how I'll be finished soon, how I'll have more money, then I feel happy. Other days, my head hurts and I think I'll be gone by tomorrow. I cry for my daughters. What will they do? My sister has seven kids and lots of grandchildren, she can't take them in. My mother's old and any day now she'll die. I've had so much sorrow. I lost my husband, I lost my dad, my daughters have a terrible life. I want to leave and never come back.'

'Here, Perla.' The dog nestles at Alicia's feet and Alicia picks her up.

'My daughters are my only hope,' says Rosa. 'Alicia's hard-working, she's clever and she's a good student. I want her to have a proper job and make something of herself, not like me.'

Alicia works at night in the mine because that way she can still go to school in the morning. She doesn't want to give up school. If she is to escape from the mine and take her mother and her sister to a flat in town, she has to study and find work.

'What do you want to be when you're older, Alicia?'

'A doctor.'

'Why?'

'To cure the children on the Cerro for free.' She smiles faintly. 'But sometimes I fall asleep at school.'

* * *

I go home and write an article about Alicia and other kids who work in the mine.

Over the following months I call every now and then. I talk to Rosa a couple of times and to Alicia once, but the line is always bad and the conversations are short. Often, the phone is out of charge or there's no coverage. I stop calling but I still get updates from Cecilia Molina, the director of Cepromin. In one of her messages, she tells me that the children and adolescents who work in the Cerro Rico mines have set up an association. They held a meeting and took a vote: they made Alicia president.

2

The Princess
and The Baron

Two years pass before I return to Bolivia.

I don't go straight to Potosí. I travel by bus from La Paz to Oruro, where I will visit the Simón Patiño Museum, which celebrates the miner who put a stick of dynamite in just the right place and became the fifth-richest man in the world. I am also going to interview Dora Camacho, the president of the committee of miners' housewives, the ones who overthrew a military dictatorship and now have to put up with the mockery of the miners every time they try to speak at their rallies.

From Oruro, I catch another bus south to Llallagua. Up here on the high plateau, at an altitude of 3,800 metres, it feels more like a ship than a motor vehicle. Lulled by the gentle rocking motion, I have a vague sensation that we are moving forwards but the view through the window is unchanging: a dusty brown plain and a whitish blue sky. The impression of ocean travel is reinforced by the vehicle's slow pace and the roar of the engine, as if it were struggling to make headway against the waves.

It's because of the altitude. At almost 4,000 metres above the level of an unimaginable sea, the atmosphere is very thin. On the high plateau, the engine takes in far less oxygen than it would at sea level. With so little oxygen, the engine burns less fuel and generates less power. To compensate, the engine needs to take in more air and the crankshaft has to revolve at a far higher speed, a struggle for progress that is hard not to read as a metaphor for the challenges faced by Bolivia throughout its history.

* * *

I once caught a flight from La Paz to Cochabamba to interview Gregorio Iriarte, the Priest of the Mines, and the cabin crew gave the usual safety briefing, even telling us to don our life jackets if we fell into the sea. Although it was a domestic flight, they stood there with arms outstretched to signal the exits, put their life jackets on and simulated inflating them. It was as if we were recreating the phantom sea, feeling it to be Bolivian in the same way that they say an amputee still feels a missing limb, and by the time the explanations were over I wanted to jump from my seat and shout, 'Bolivia, from the mountains to the ocean, *carajo*!' But the country definitively renounced all such claims in a treaty of 1904, in large part because it suited the mining oligarchs, who ignored any interests other than their own. In return, Chile allowed them to construct a railway line to carry their ore to the coast. So the country agreed to be hemmed in and never to raise the issue again and found itself condemned to isolation and poverty, so long as the mine trains could reach the sea. An abundance of raw materials has often been a curse for the weak countries where they are found. The owners of the materials take possession of the country and wealth simply becomes another cause of poverty.

* * *

The bus veers round towards the east and points its prow at a series of humps on the horizon. From a distance, it looks like a modest range of hills, but soon the road is snaking its way through narrow gorges, plunging into deep valleys, skirting the edge of steep ravines. Sun, wind and ice pulverize the slopes, and torrential rain washes them away. Piece by piece, the mountains are dissolving into the plain.

* * *

In Llallagua they hollowed out the mountains and created new ones. They extracted millions of tons of rock, separated out the small portion that contained valuable minerals, and tipped the rest into the valleys. Now the road winds through this arid chain of natural hills and artificial slag heaps, and from a distance it is hard to distinguish one from the other.

Close up, the differences are easier to spot. While there is nobody on the hills, men and women walk slowly across the heaps, their eyes to the ground. They bend down, pick up a piece of rock, inspect it, toss it aside or, occasionally, put it in a bag. The slag heaps are made up of the rock that was discarded during decades of industrial mining because the ore content was so low that extracting it was not profitable. But now, for many families, the only way to obtain a little money is to break these rocks into pieces with a hammer in search of a few grams of tin.

The town of Llallagua, in the department of Potosí, lies at the foot of the mountain that contains the richest seam of tin ever found. It was the heartland of Bolivian trade unionism, the setting for the nationalization of the mines, clandestine guerrilla movements, military massacres and strikes that toppled dictators, until the movement fell apart following the privatizations of 1986. The miners atomized into a thousand small-scale cooperatives, and the trade union, the political vanguard and everything else evaporated overnight.

The political change was dramatic and, among Llallagua's pyramids of slag, the Bolivian child workers' movement was born.

'When I was mayor, I was asked if there were children working in the mines and I said no. I really thought that was the case. I just didn't see them.' I am talking to Héctor Soliz, a man in his late forties, whose centre parting and round glasses give him the air of a schoolteacher.

We are talking in a teashop in Llallagua, in the centre of a town that was once the heart of the Bolivian mining industry, then was devastated by economic collapse and almost abandoned, but has now come to life again. It has 40,000 inhabitants, of whom 8,000 are students at a university which specializes in mining engineering but also teaches medicine, nursing and social sciences.

The town is a cluster of low houses, huddled on a gentle slope at an altitude of 3,900 metres at the foot of a mountain with two hump-shaped peaks. They say the mountain looks like a giant tuber and that the town is named after *Llallawa*, the Andean spirit of the potato crop. Thousands of people came to this wasteland of barren stone in search of abundance: not of potatoes, which are small and low-yielding in the local soil, but of one of the richest tin deposits on the planet. Just over 100 years ago, the miner Simón Patiño placed his dynamite in exactly the right spot and struck the legendary seam. Houses built of adobe bricks soon sprang up to accommodate the newcomers, and the town was born.

'I became mayor in 2000, and the people from Cepromin asked for a meeting,' Soliz recalls. 'They told me the International Labour Organization was recording the worst forms of child labour, such as mining. That's why they came to see me. And I told them we really didn't have any kids in the mines here.'

Cepromin conducted a census in the Siglo XX mining district, home to 7,200 people, and after a few months it published the results: the survey identified 147 boys and 28 girls who worked in the mining industry. Of these, 42 boys and one girl worked inside the mine, with the remaining children performing tasks on the outside. They worked to supplement their family incomes or to replace parents who had died, been injured or fallen ill.

'These kids start at nine or ten years of age, just helping out. At first, they undertake simple tasks: they sweep the *canchamina*, collecting any pieces of ore-bearing rock, taking food and water to the miners. Then they move on to other tasks: breaking up the rocks with mallets, grinding them down, and gradually they take on heavier work until eventually they go underground. So what happens? Because they're kids helping their families, we don't realize they're working. They don't earn a wage, so they're not workers. That was our mentality back then.'

Cepromin developed a successful programme to get children out of the mine. It focused on the parents, providing vocational training and affordable credit to help them learn a trade or set up a food business so they would have a more reliable source of income. Cepromin also invested in an industrial mill so that the miners and their children wouldn't have to spend their time (and destroy their health) crushing the rock by hand. Profits rose and the parents no longer needed the help of their children. Within a few months, eighty families had stopped sending their children to the mine.

But the success was fragile. When tin prices collapsed, some miners turned to their children again to help them work longer shifts and meet their targets.

The situation in Llallagua has improved: there are fewer children in the mines. But the crux of the problem remains. So long as there is poverty, there will be child labour.

The Cepromin project also organized libraries, literacy classes and computer courses, and workshops on public speaking, self-esteem and citizens' rights. Young people had time to think about something other than work and began to have other ideas.

For example: demanding their right to work.

They set up their own organization (NATS, which stands for Working Children and Adolescents), they wrote letters to the authorities to report cases of exploitation, and they challenged the rules of the ILO (which funds Cepromin's projects and prohibits work by those aged under fourteen). Instead, they argued that they should not be prevented from working, because they needed the money if they weren't to starve. They fought for years and they won: in 2014 the Bolivian government changed the law and allowed young people to work from the age of ten.

'In middle-class families, nobody would dream of saying that children have the right to work. It's only something poor people would demand,' I had been told a couple of years earlier by Eva Udaeta, director of the Plan for the Progressive Eradication of Child Labour, at the Bolivian Ministry of Employment. 'How can we defend the right to something that is reserved for the very poorest and would be unthinkable for the rest of society?'

Udaeta recognized that her plan lacked resources – they could barely organize a few awareness-raising workshops and send a handful of employment inspectors to mines across the country – but she argued that the government of Evo Morales was the first to have established a programme to eradicate child labour and that it was tackling the underlying issue of child poverty.

Bolivia has just lived through a boom period. From 2004 to 2014, the economy grew at an annual rate of 5 per cent, driven by rising volumes of gas, mineral and oil exports and high prices for these commodities. In the course of ten years, per capita income tripled, rising from 978 to 3,077 dollars per year (an average figure, which says nothing of the huge gap between rich and poor in one of the world's most unequal countries).

The money was rolling in and the Morales government, which came to power in 2006, directed its distribution. Gas, oil and mining operations were nationalized, as were some electricity and telecommunications companies, with a portion of the profits being channelled into targeted social benefits. The Juana Azurduy Bond – worth just over 300 dollars, in several instalments – is paid to mothers throughout their pregnancy and during the first two years of the baby's life if they attend medical check-ups, which are designed to help reduce maternal and infant mortality. Primary and secondary school students receive the Juancito Pinto Bond – worth about thirty dollars per year – if they attend class and complete their studies, a condition designed to reduce drop-out rates. Those over the age of sixty are eligible for the Dignity Income, worth almost 500 dollars per year for those who don't have a pension and 400 dollars for those who do. In 2015, the Bolivian minimum salary was raised to 275 dollars per month.

During the boom years, there were more jobs and higher pay. Old people, students, pregnant women and babies – a third of all Bolivians – received money from the state. As a result, the spectacular rise in the country's income translated into a spectacular reduction in poverty rates, which fell from 63 to 39 per cent. And extreme poverty, affecting people who could not even be sure where their next meal was coming from, fell from 38 to 17 per cent. The country also saw some of the biggest reductions in levels of inequality between rich and poor.

In 2014, the prices of oil, gas and other raw materials began to fall. Morales has been criticized for basing poverty reduction on direct payments sustained by the boom, while failing to invest in long-term plans to develop the economy to reduce the country's dependency on commodities. This is the complaint in Potosí: that, while the mining sector saw its income multiply by a factor of ten and the state paid out social benefits, the government failed to build hospitals, schools, roads and airports.

And it passed legislation to allow people to work from the age of ten. 'That was a real blow,' Soliz recalls. 'When the kids started to hold meetings and draw up their demands, I thought they'd ask for study grants and family support so they wouldn't have to work. But that's exactly what they asked for: to work. They said that if they weren't allowed to work they'd starve. That they'd work with or without the protection of the law but that they'd carry on working. It made me think. Forbidding youngsters from working is pointless if their families are in poverty. What else can they do? Now I think we need to legalize it but subject it to strict controls so that working doesn't damage children's health, their education or their development; so that the bosses can't exploit them. I know this means accepting a lesser evil while we solve the big problem.'

In Llallagua, just like in Cerro Rico de Potosí, the big problem is poverty. In Llallagua, just like in Cerro Rico de Potosí, they discovered one of the richest deposits on the planet.

* * *

In 1900, a dynamite explosion revealed a wall of shiny rock.

According to legend, the first words uttered by the owner of the deposit, a fortune hunter by the name of Simón Patiño, were, 'For the love of God, don't let it be silver!'

Patiño had purchased four hectares in Llallagua from a penniless miner who had failed to recover enough ore to cover his costs. Patiño hired half a dozen labourers and put them to work digging and laying dynamite. The charge that transformed the history of Bolivia was laid by four workers named Muruchi, González, Miranda and Frías, according to Patiño's biographer, Roberto Querejazu.

With silver prices in the doldrums, Patiño was hoping for tin, a metal that is often found in association with silver-bearing ores but which the miners of the colonial period had ignored. Nobody had been interested in tin but, at the start of the twentieth century, industry in Europe and North America was consuming it in ever larger quantities. A malleable metal often used in alloys, tin is ideal for coating other metals such as steel to protect them from friction and corrosion. It is used for soldering, to manufacture tin plate, and in the production of food cans, ball bearings, tinfoil, computer circuits and armaments.

Demand was high and supply was limited. Patiño used his savings to buy up as much land as he could on the nearby slopes before the news got out. The bet paid off because the deposit turned out to be huge. It was called La Salvadora: the Saviour. Mining engineer Jorge Espinoza has calculated that the vein was 200 metres long, 70 metres high and 2 metres wide, containing some 131,600 tons of tin, worth 967 million dollars. Patiño extracted this wealth in just two years.

He hired dozens of miners and accommodated them in huts at Uncía, at the foot of the deposit. He built a road to transport the ore to the railway that connects Bolivia to the Chilean coast, enabling him to export the tin. In the nearby city of Oruro, he built a palace for his family, established his company headquarters and founded the

Banco Mercantil. He equipped the mine with the latest technology: huge German engines to generate electricity to power the drills, air compressors to ventilate the galleries, a mine railway to haul the rock, elevators to carry the miners underground. He also built a plant to process the ore before it was exported.

The Argentine writer Jaime Molins visited the site in 1915.

Pulled by a German-built Imperator locomotive, the convoy of twenty wagons snaked its way like a serpent to the mouth of the mine. The wagons were unloaded at the station and the convoy disappeared back inside the earth.

The plant at Uncía is the most modern and efficient in the whole country. There, we saw six crushing mills, three grinding machines, Kauffman gyratory ovens, electric coolers, washing tables, a magnetic separator, and wet and dry concentration devices. In the engine department, we found five petrol-powered Diesel engines, which generate electricity for the plant, the mine and the settlement of Uncía. We visited workshops, dynamite stores, the playing field and the bowling alley. We also saw the pharmacy and the hospital.

Uncía has 10,000 inhabitants. The houses are clustered together without any kind of plan. The town is full of small businesses operated by Syrians,

Austrians, Italians, Spaniards and the occasional Frenchman. Patiño's company has a general store for its workers. There is a sub-prefecture, a municipality, a theatre, a public market, schools, a hotel and even a weekly newspaper with its own printshop.

Molins also entered the mine. He described it as an anthill, the galleries teeming with hundreds of workers running this way and that, sweating and grunting. He was deafened by the thunder of compressed air drills, the screech of winches, the throb of air compressors, the blast of dynamite, the underground blacksmith's forge where the embers glowed like blood and showers of stars shot from the anvil at each blow of the hammer.

* * *

Today, the showers of stars pierce the corneas of the miners of Llallagua. One of them is waiting in the eye clinic, which is staffed by Cuban doctors and is housed in the old mansion that Patiño built at the foot of the mountain. The miner is seated, his chin resting on his chest. When he raises his head, he winces with pain and his right eye is awash with blood. A tiny chip of stone has lodged itself in his eye. It's a common accident in the mine, but one that could be prevented by the simplest of measures: safety goggles.

But there are no safety measures, either simple or complex, in the former Patiño mines. The workers extract the tin using artisanal methods. They make holes with a hammer and chisel, insert the sticks of dynamite, set them off, gather the fallen rock with shovels, load it into sacks, carry burdens of forty or fifty kilos back up to the surface, and break the rock into pieces to separate out the valuable parts. There is no electricity, no engines or drills, no trains or processing plants. The technology is more primitive than it was a hundred years ago.

When one of the miners gets an eye injury, they go to the eye clinic in the old mansion. Patiño, the Tin Baron, had this extravagant building erected a stone's throw from the mine entrance. It is a long mustard-coloured pavilion with arched windows, topped off by a Scots baronial tower. Apart from the clinic, the rest of the building is given over to a ghostly museum, with forty-six empty rooms, empty salons and courtyards, and an empty ballroom beneath a glass roof. Some years ago the ruined building was saved and restored, and now the main rooms house a few curiosities for unlikely tourists: an English carriage in which Patiño and his wife used to go for rides, a statue of the Tío, some old documents in display cabinets, a few mining hammers, and a spanner so vast that its jaws could enclose a human neck.

The mansion is full of echoes.

Nearby stands the Miraflores plant, a huge shed that still houses the five diesel engines – each the size of a lorry – brought from Germany by Patiño in 1901 to supply the mines with electricity. The engines stopped running for the last time in 1986, when the state abandoned the mines, and since then they have been accumulating grime in this dilapidated warehouse which the local council hopes to convert into a museum and cafeteria. For the moment, the only visitors are the rats that scurry across the floor and the pigeons that flutter among the rafters.

Hector Soliz shows me up a staircase so we can look down on the engines from above.

'I suspect it's a myth, but they say General Electric only made these engines for two customers: Patiño and the *Titanic*.'

For Patiño and the *Titanic*.

The ruins of the processing plant also remain, the furnaces where the ore was heated to separate out the impurities, and into which the corpses of several miners were thrown after the massacre of 1923. It was one of the early massacres, one of the first clashes between ranks of miners and ranks of soldiers, dynamite against shrapnel, a massacre that had been brewing since the Uncía strike of 1918, the first miners' strike in South America, which Bolivia's rulers – terrified by the prospect of the spread of Bolshevism – repressed with a state of siege that lasted for twenty-two months. And Uncía and Llallagua were labelled 'Soviet towns'.

Today, there are just a few miners – their hands stained purple with tin dust – walking back down the mountain to Miraflores. The old black-and-white photographs show the miners' houses, the company offices, the stores, the theatre. If you shift your gaze from the photos back to the town, it is as if the place had been hit by an atomic bomb: a scene of ruined buildings, crumbling walls, rubbish tips, piles of rubble. The mining families have chosen the least damaged houses and have patched the holes with cardboard and sheets of metal. In the streets, chickens peck in the dirt, an emaciated dog ambles past, a boy watches over a dozen sheep grazing among the ruins of the empire.

* * *

Patiño's wealth soon exceeded that of the entire country. In 1906, he founded the Banco Mercantil with capital of over a million pounds sterling, more than the national budget and twice the combined equity of all Bolivia's other banks.

And the best was still to come.

Following the outbreak of the First World War, the arms factories of Europe and North American paid top dollar for thousands of tons of ore at a time when Bolivia had become one of the leading producers of tin, bismuth, wolfram and antimony. It could have been an extraordinary opportunity to develop the country.

Patiño's millions continued to multiply, as did those of the other Bolivian mining barons, Carlos Víctor Aramayo and Mauricio Hochschild. The three constituted the oligarchy that dominated the country's political system, chose governments, dictated laws, exported the raw material, kept workers in conditions of semi-slavery, found ways to dodge paying tax in Bolivia ... and kept their fortunes overseas.

Patiño bought up the country's largest mines in a few years. In secret, using intermediary companies, he gradually bought shares in a Chilean firm that owned large deposits in Bolivia. In 1924, after he had acquired two-thirds of the equity, he turned up at a meeting of shareholders in Santiago, took control of the firm and, according to legend, shouted 'Viva Bolivia!'

He presented the operation as a patriotic act, the recovery of Bolivia's wealth from the Chileans, the same hated Chileans who, just a few years before, had deprived Bolivia of its outlet to the sea.

But Patiño's patriotism does not appear to have been particularly intense. By that time, he had been living in a mansion in Paris for the previous twelve years. And when he took possession of the Chilean companies, he brought all of his mines and railways together under the name Patiño Mines and registered the holding in Delaware, USA, a tax haven which continues to be used today by large companies eager to evade billions of dollars in tax. Aramayo transferred his company to Switzerland while Hochschild relocated to Chile.

From his Delaware office, Patiño began to expand across the globe. He never built his own tin smelter in Bolivia. Instead, he travelled to Great Britain to buy Williams, Harvey and Company, the world's largest smelter at the time. He followed up this purchase with seven more. He also acquired mines in Indonesia, Malaysia, the Netherlands, Nigeria and Thailand. He controlled half of global tin production and in 1925 his annual income (50 million pesos) was only slightly lower than that of the whole of Bolivia.

In 1927, the *New York Times* ranked him the fifth-wealthiest man in the world, behind Ford, Rockefeller, Zaharoff and Vanderbilt, but ahead of Rothschild and Guggenheim.

* * *

'The borer, the highest paid member of the team, receives two Bolivian pesos a day,' Cochabamba's *El Comercio* newspaper reported at the start of the twentieth century.

He works a ten-hour shift, hundreds of metres below ground, making holes in the rock in which to place four or five sticks of dynamite. He breathes in metal-bearing dust that destroys his lungs with silicosis. He works half naked, acidic water dripping onto his body. He has to descend hundreds of metres on precarious ladders. He crawls through tunnels that could collapse at any moment. He runs the risk of being blown to pieces by a faulty stick of dynamite. He never sees the light of day and his way is illuminated instead by the opaque yellow glow of a tallow lamp. His clothing is reduced to rags, which are eaten away by acid. He lacks air and space. Of his daily wage of two pesos, he spends 60 cents on three sticks of dynamite, 10 cents on a guide, 25 cents on tallow for his lamp, 10 more on coca leaf, 10 on bread, 5 on cigarettes and 20 on wine and brandy. A total of one peso 40 cents. Leaving him 60 cents per day to feed and clothe his family.

Viva Bolivia!

Extraordinary managerial skills, commercial insight and investment in foreign engineers, modern machinery and transport networks were the keys to Patiño's wealth, according to the historian Herbert S. Klein.

The historian Juan Albarracín identifies another factor: 'Without the Indians of the *altiplano*, the tin mining industry of the twentieth century would not have prospered.'

Bolivian miners worked long shifts: twelve, fourteen, eighteen, even twenty-four hours. A whole day and night underground, hacking at the stone without respite, racked by hunger and sustained only by coca leaves. Their salaries barely allowed them to subsist, they were decimated by accident and disease, there was no insurance, no pensions and no record of injuries. 'In the mining camps, the only rule was that exercised by the company manager, without freedoms or constitutional guarantees,' writes Albarracín.

Who was going to stand up for the miners? Patiño had an army of politicians, judges, lawyers, journalists, bankers, generals and even presidents on his private payroll, and many of these also held generously remunerated positions in the mining companies. They issued laws that favoured

Patiño, they outlawed the unions, they arrested and exiled the workers' leaders and, if there was any sign of protests or strikes, they sent the army into the mining camps. The results were the Avicaya massacre in 1905, the Amayapampa massacre in 1911, the Monte Blanco massacre in 1914, the Uncía massacre in 1923. 'The Indians had no citizenship rights,' explains Albarracín. 'The mining companies could never have accumulated so much capital without first suffocating democracy in Bolivia.'

Very occasionally, a minister or even a president dared to criticize the privileges of the mining barons, to denounce them for evading taxes and for opposing any law designed to improve the lives of ordinary Bolivians if it wasn't to their liking. These ministers and presidents didn't last long. When President Gutiérrez Guerra proposed a law to tax the mining industry, the barons acted as one: they stopped paying the government the hard currency they owed it in export duties, thus pushing the country to the brink of bankruptcy, and amid the ensuing chaos a *coup d'état* deposed Gutiérrez Guerra and installed Bautista Saavedra, a caudillo supported by Aramayo. The mining magnates formed shifting alliances, seeking to place their preferred lawyers and generals in power, and as a result throughout the first half of the twentieth century Bolivia was shaken by a succession of coups sponsored by the mining oligarchs.

'Patiño is a destroyer of presidents,' wrote the sociologist José Antonio Arze in 1939, 'he is a state within the state. He fixes elections and funds coups against any government that refuses to do his bidding.'

At the same time, Patiño presented himself as a saviour of the fatherland, providing work for thousands and lending money to a country that was constantly on the verge of bankruptcy. In exchange, of course, for the approval of certain laws and certain projects that suited his interests. For example, he granted the government a loan of 600,000 pounds sterling to extend the rail network – exactly the network that he needed to export ore – in exchange for a commitment not to raise the duties on tin. These duties were derisory (between 3 and 5 per cent) and were not even collected in full. Instead, as Albarracín explains, the state allowed Patiño to commit massive fraud.

The Bolivian customs service had no idea how much ore was leaving the country. The state didn't monitor exports, contenting itself instead with collecting 3 per cent of the profits booked by Patiño upon selling the Bolivian ore on the London market, after refining it at his smelter in Liverpool. The state calculated how much tax was due on the basis of reports issued by Patiño's companies, which inflated the costs and manipulated the revenue figures so that the profit would appear to be lower. Albarracín calculates that the combination of accounting tricks and smuggling on a huge scale meant that Bolivia collected less than 1 per cent of the value of its ore. And business owners didn't pay tax on income or capital transfers either.

Patiño, Hochschild and Aramayo worked their miners to the bone, extracted all of the country's raw material and shipped it abroad without leaving so much as a few crumbs in Bolivia. During the first three decades of the twentieth century, the phenomenal income from tin gave Bolivia a unique opportunity to develop, an opportunity that would never come again, but the country's wealth accumulated in Delaware, London and Geneva – just as the riches from silver had accumulated in colonial Spain – and none of it remained in Bolivia. Instead, the whole country was organized like a vast mining camp: a few processing plants at the mines, the railways and roads necessary to export the ore, two or three cities where the families of a rich and exclusive elite were housed in small, select neighbourhoods, to which 'Indians' were denied entry except to work as cooks, waiters or domestic servants. Outside of these oases of privilege, the country was mired in poverty, lacking schools, hospitals, roads, industry or commerce; the population, illiterate and lacking the right to vote, suffered starvation and brutal repression. Daniel Salamanca, the country's president from 1931 to 1934, put ruling-class assumptions about the passivity of the masses into words with the infamous phrase 'One could sow turnips on the backs of Bolivians'.

But the barons did build some beautiful mansions.

* * *

Three Chilean ladies enter Simón Patiño's palace in Oruro. Around sixty years of age, they wear trouser suits and have pearl necklaces, pearl bracelets and pearl earrings. They tell the guide that two of them are cousins, and distant descendants of the Tin Baron.

'Bolivia owes so much to Patiño, so much,' sighs one of the cousins. 'There should be a statue to him in the main square of every town in the country.'

The ladies are very friendly and they are delighted when they see me taking notes during the tour. 'How marvellous! Look at that lad. Foreigners appreciate our history more than we do ourselves. We have no idea how much our countries owe to men like Patiño.' They congratulate me and ask what I do, and when I tell them I'm a journalist they encourage me to write all about Patiño.

The guide tells us the legend of how Patiño found the largest tin deposit in the world, how he gave jobs to thousands of workers, established banks and built railways. And he was just a mestizo from Cochabamba who was born into poverty but became one of the richest men on the planet.

In 1900, shortly after finding the La Salvadora seam, Patiño brought a group of French architects to Oruro to build this two-floor neoclassical mansion in the middle of town, where he installed himself and his family. A grand stairway leads up to the first floor, which houses the armoury, the hall of mirrors, the games room, the music room, the solarium, the nursery, the sauna, the dispensary and the bedrooms. A gilded Christ with a heart of bronze presides over the chapel, which also contains a golden chalice, a Roman Bible, a set of gold leaf candlesticks, some porcelain flower vases and the chasuble embroidered with gold and silver thread that was once worn by the resident priest.

The displays include silver armour, Persian rugs, cabinets inlaid with ivory images from China, bamboo and wickerwork chairs from India, a grandfather clock with a gold pendulum, a dinner service of French porcelain, marble tables, desks inlaid with silver, gold-plated chandeliers, pianos adorned with silver and bronze engravings, a Stradivarius cello, and an electric *orquestón* (a cabinet capable of reproducing the sounds of an entire orchestra at the press of a button) which had been commissioned in Hamburg.

And the statue of a black child.

'It's Salvador, Patiño's talisman,' the guide explains.

When Patiño was working the Llallagua find without success and was close to bankruptcy, his wife, Albina, sold her jewels and left Oruro to join him at the mine and bring him the money he needed to pay the wages he owed his labourers. Along the way, Albina found an abandoned black child, a four-year-old orphan, and she took him with her to Llallagua.

'The kid brought them luck. Patiño found the seam and called it La Salvadora. And he called the boy Salvador.'

In 1931, Patiño created a foundation that still exists today. It funds a centre for Bolivian university students in Switzerland, a paediatric hospital and an organic farm in Cochabamba, and three cultural centres in La Paz,

Cochabamba and Santa Cruz. In Bolivia, you can visit four of the Tin Baron's palaces: there are two in Cochabamba, this one in Oruro and another in Uncía.

There are no statues in town squares.

* * *

The Chaquimayo river stinks. It trickles down the slope, hemmed in by the steep sides of a gully, and runs through town like an open sewer. Near the top of the hill, the miners separate out the ore in pools of water mixed with xanthate: the earth and gravel sink to the bottom while the tin floats. The ore is skimmed off the surface and the pools empty into the Chaquimayo: thousands of litres of water and xanthate, a toxic substance that is a compound of carbon disulphide, potassium hydroxide and alcohol. By the time the river reaches the town, it is a murky stream topped with yellow scum and the water accumulates in lime-green puddles along the way. The banks are littered with plastic and rusty metal, and a dog's corpse buzzes with flies.

I walk across a bridge with Héctor Soliz. He tells me two things: that *chaquimayo* means 'dry river' in Quechua and that the river marks an old boundary. We are leaving Llallagua proper and entering Siglo XX, Simón Patiño's private camp, formerly only accessible to the company's employees. In the beginning, there were only the mines and the camp. Then the merchants came and built their houses, their shops, their canteens, their stores, to supply the thousands of miners who worked for Patiño. The town of Llallagua grew up to serve Siglo XX. The company erected a fence around the camp and closed off the entrance with a barrier, of which the remains are still visible: two metal posts, one at each side of the road.

Patiño was ahead of his time. The name he gave to this camp – surrounded by fences and barriers – was Siglo XX: the twentieth century.

He chose the name because he thought it had a modern ring but he can hardly have imagined how apt it would be: the camp was a synthesis of Bolivia's century. It was here that the key episodes of the country's politics were decided. The early capitalism of the mining barons, the 1952 revolution, the nationalization of the mines, the coups, Che Guevara's guerrilla insurgency, the army massacres, the strikes that overthrew dictators, and now the political movement of child workers.

This is all that's left of Siglo XX, all that's left of the twentieth century: poisoned soil, a clutch of tumbledown houses, families that don't have enough to eat, children who work in the mines.

It's easy to find them on Saturdays.

Today is Saturday, and Soliz takes me to places that crop up time and time again in the now legendary tales of strikes, revolutions and massacres. In the Plaza del Minero – Miner's Square – stands a huge bronze statue of the trade unionist Federico Escóbar speaking to the masses, and another statue of a miner on top of a mountain, his chest bare and muscular, a drill in one hand, a rifle held high above his head in the other. Here is the building that houses the Catholic radio station, Radio Pius XII, and over there are the offices of the communist trade union: rival headquarters during the Cold War. This is no metaphor: the walls are still scarred by explosions and pocked with bullet holes.

The mining camp has the geometry and the function of a beehive. It is formed by row upon row of squat adobe houses. One row of houses and another row of houses and another and another and another. Some are little more than ruins, the very ground on which they stand collapsing beneath them.

'Since Comibol left, the miners work where they want, without any kind of plan,' Soliz says. Comibol (the Mining Corporation of Bolivia) is the state enterprise that was in charge of the country's mineral deposits from the 1952 revolution until 1986, when it went bust and abandoned all the mines except one. Now the miners work in cooperatives, using the most rudimentary of methods, with only the most basic technology and with no engineers to decide where they can dig. They drill wherever they want to, and sometimes they don't realize there's another gallery right above them, and the roof falls in. Or they drill close to the houses and the ground collapses.

Today is Saturday, a day for crushing stones.

On the outskirts of the camp, women lay sheets of canvas on the ground. They tip wheelbarrow-loads of stones onto the canvas and spread them out. This is the rock the miners have extracted during the week and now it's time to hammer it, to crush it, to crumble it into pieces, to grind it down. This work used to be performed by machines, by the mills that Patiño built and which later passed into Comibol ownership. Since 1986, when the government closed the mills, the families of Siglo XX have crushed the rock using the same technology as the Incas: mallets and quern-stones.

The women, the *palliris*, sit on the ground. They are wearing bowler hats, dusty knitted jackets, skirts of several layers, and gumboots. They place the first chunk of stone on a large, flat rock that serves as an anvil, lift a heavy mallet and crack the piece of stone like a nut. They put the tin-bearing fragments in a bag and discard the rest. They break one stone, then another, then another. Sometimes they hit a finger by mistake. Their hands are deformed, the fingers swollen, bent and dry like the twisted pods of locust beans, the nails black with dried blood.

Soliz greets one of the women, introduces her to me and explains why I'm here. She looks up at me and is dazzled slightly by the sun. She smiles and says, 'We *palliris*, we work so hard.'

She arches her back a little, picks up the next stone and strikes it with the mallet.

In this part of the camp there are fifteen to twenty women breaking stones. Some of them are old at forty, their faces burnt, with warts, missing teeth, crooked backs. Others are young mothers, scarcely more than teenagers, who hammer while their babies crawl happily among the rocks, their faces covered with snot and dust. A three-year-old girl pushes a plastic car along the ground.

There are boys carrying buckets of water, girls selling soft drinks, biscuits and sweets, women frying *salteñas* – pasties with a spicy filling of meat and egg – and the occasional staggering, shouting drunk, who is ignored by everyone. Tiny feet and little heads plastered with sweaty hair protrude from the colourful blankets tied to the backs of some of the women.

A couple of lads aged fifteen or sixteen come to collect two sacks which one of the *palliris* has filled with tin-bearing fragments. They lift the sacks onto their backs and carry them fifty metres to a flat piece of ground, above which floats a cloud of blue dust.

'These kids normally go to school,' says Soliz, 'but at the weekend they help with the grinding.'

The two teenagers spill the contents of the sacks onto a sheet of metal and start to grind the rock with a *quimbalete*, an enormous roller the shape of a half-moon, full of concrete and stones. It must weigh half a ton. Each of the lads grasps the roller by the handle at either end, and they begin to rock it, up and down, up and down, up and down. The stones crumble and are gradually reduced to a fine layer of grey gravel. They work over it again.

'The *quimbalete* is really heavy. If they use it for a long time they end up with sore backs. And sometimes one of them crushes his feet.'

The grey sand is mixed with water and xanthate in deep trays. Five men with rubber gloves perform the task. They put a hand into the tray and stir the liquid, which gives off a smell of rotten cauliflower. Foam containing the particles of tin begins to form, and this is skimmed off before the remaining liquid is tipped into a channel that runs into the Chaquimayo. The smell is overpowering. Carbon disulphide, one of the components of xanthate, passes from the lungs into the bloodstream almost immediately. Small doses are enough to cause the first symptoms: headaches, dizziness, exhaustion and inflammation of the skin, throat and eyes. If you inhale it for longer, it can damage your heart, your kidneys and your liver; it can make your blood pressure rise and causes depression, amnesia and psychosis. Extended exposure can kill you.

As I walk around, the stench of decay penetrates my brain and solidifies between my temples.

The high price they pay for working here is plain to see, but how much do they earn?

'It depends on the wars,' says Soliz. 'During the wars in Iraq and Afghanistan, they made good money. Because the United States bought a lot of tin to manufacture weapons, and the price went up.'

In 2001, the average price of tin was just 2.03 dollars per pound: a pittance. It wasn't even enough to cover costs, so lots of people abandoned the mine and Llallagua lost inhabitants. They moved to the cities to look for work or went back to their villages to grow potatoes and rear sheep, because lots of Bolivian miners are peasants who look for additional income in the mines when the price of tin rises.

In the years that followed, prices shot up, reaching a peak of 12.10 dollars in 2012. And the miners came back to Llallagua.

The sharp increase began in 2006, driven primarily by events in China and Indonesia, the world's two largest tin producers. During the 1990s, China flooded the market and prices fell. Then, during the first decade of the new millennium, Chinese industry grew so fast that the country became a net importer of tin, and prices went up. Eventually, though, prices began to fall again and by 2015 tin was trading at around 7 dollars per pound.

The miners are at the mercy of this international roller-coaster. A miner in a large private company such as San Cristóbal earns around 700 dollars, while one of the miners working for a cooperative makes anything from 150 to 700 dollars depending on how well or badly the month has gone. The cooperative member takes his load to an agent in one of the warehouses in Llallagua, and the agent weighs and analyses the ore and pays the miner in cash.

From Llallagua, the tin is taken by truck to Oruro. From there it travels by train to Chile and then onwards by boat to China, India, Japan, South Korea or the United States. Many months later it may make it back to Llallagua transformed, for example, into a sardine can.

*   *   *

On Sunday I head out of Llallagua. The huts gradually become fewer and, after ten minutes, I am walking across a deserted plain, the ground the colour of cinnamon, bisected by the black line of the road and the white line of an orderly flock of sheep being hurried along by a boy.

The river churns with earth and foam. Up here, almost 4,000 metres above sea level, I think about the course it will follow, how the poison and the memory of the poison will gradually be diluted. The Chaquimayo is a tributary of the Pilcomayo, which is a tributary of the Paraguay, which is a tributary of the Paraná, which is a tributary of the Rio de la Plata. And the Rio de la Plata flows into the Atlantic Ocean, the same ocean whose waves break on Zurriola beach in my home town of San Sebastián in the Spanish Basque Country. Back at home we neither know nor care.

On this plain outside Llallagua, three or four families have set up a rudimentary operation on the banks of the Chaquimayo. Tubes divert the river water into small pools which are covered with planks and have small wooden sluice gates. The waste water has been discarded by the miners but still carries some ore, and these families filter it with fine sieves or *maritates*. There are men digging ditches, shovelling mounds of gravel, hauling sacks, pushing wheelbarrows. And there's a ten-year-old girl, in a tracksuit and baseball cap, squatting next to the pool. She puts her bare hands in the brown water, scrapes the bottom and digs out handfuls of sand. These are the last particles of Llallagua's tin.

The particles that the girl salvages from the toxic water with her bare hands are put in a sack, taken by truck to Oruro, by train to Chile and by boat to China, and some of these particles may reach my house, close to Zurriola beach, transformed, for example, into a sardine can, and we neither know nor care.

* * *

On Monday I catch a bus from Llallagua that finally takes me back to Potosí, two years after my previous visit. From the window, I see that Cerro Rico is still standing. It hasn't collapsed, because the Bolivian government has filled in the cracks at the summit with 50,000 tons of earth and cement at a cost of more than half a million dollars. The adobe huts on the Cerro Rico are also still there because nobody has spent a cent on the people who live in them.

When I get back to Potosí I learn that Alicia is president, that she has a study grant, that she's making her way through high school, that she is no longer a slave of the miners. Cepromin paid off part of her mother's debt, the cooperative cancelled some of it, and a fundraiser covered the rest.

On Tuesday morning I walk up to Rosa, Alicia and Evelyn's hut. It's locked and nobody's at home. There are three mine trucks and some clothes hanging on the line. I call but nobody answers in reply, no dog barks.

I go down to the Care Centre. I ask the woman on reception and she says that Alicia is in class, that she'll go and tell her right away. I ask her not to disturb Alicia, say I can come back later but the woman is already knocking on the door. She opens it and calls Alicia.

Alicia comes out into the hall and takes a moment to recognize me. Suddenly she breaks into a smile and comes up to say hello. Her hair is loose and comes down to her shoulders, and she's wearing a black leather jacket and blue jeans. She's sixteen now and her firm expression gives me the feeling I'm talking to a professional woman who has come out of her office to see what I want.

I ask how she is, how her mother and sister are, when I can go and visit them.

'Right now. I've just finished.'

She goes back into the classroom for her books and her bag and accompanies me back up the slope. I tell her I was at the hut earlier on but nobody was there, and she replies that her mother and her sister will almost certainly be with her aunt, Lorena.

'How are you doing, Alicia? How's your kidney?'

'Fine.'

'Does it give you any bother?'

'No, not any more.'

'Are you still working in the mine?'

She smiles and falls silent for a moment.

'Sometimes. The odd day. I don't tell people because everyone says I shouldn't go down the mine. All the teachers tell us we shouldn't work in the mine but sometimes I have to. The cooperative doesn't want people to know either.'

'And how are you doing at school?'

'Good. Sometimes I struggle. Sometimes I feel like giving up. But I've got to keep going.'

She wants to finish high school, get a job, earn enough money to rent a flat in town, and take her mother and her sister away from the hut. But Mum's the problem. She says she'd like to move into town but she wouldn't be able to find work there. It's tough being a guard, but what else could she do?

'And what about you? What would you like to do?'

'I don't know. Book-keeping or something like that. In a bank or an office.'

* * *

Rosa makes tea and serves it in an aluminium mug. Evelyn, now six years old, sits on the bed, eating biscuits. She's a bit shy in the presence of a stranger and she giggles and fidgets, and hums to herself. She still has warts on her hands. She comes closer when I bring out a folder with some mementos: photos from two years ago, a few copies of my article, an Italian magazine with Alicia's picture on the cover. Alicia is surprised to see herself on the front of the magazine; she laughs, then inspects the picture more closely. In the photo, she's wearing a helmet, her hair is tied back, her lips are pressed together and she stares straight at the camera. She looks tough.

* * *

'Alicia, would you like to go out for dinner? A restaurant or a pizza place? My treat. Your mum and your sister can come, too.'

'Okay ...'

She doesn't sound very convinced.

'Don't you want to? Would you rather do something else?'

We meet at five in the afternoon in Plaza 10 de Noviembre. I go into town to interview a lung specialist at the hospital, and then sit on a bench in the square to wait for Alicia, Rosa and Evelyn.

They appear, along with Aunt Lorena, her daughter Alexia, and her grandson Robertito.

We kiss on the cheeks, have our photos taken in front of the cathedral, and walk to the cinema, which is two blocks away. Three films are showing. The older women don't care what they see so Alicia chooses *Monte Carlo*, a romantic comedy about an American high school student who is mistaken for a princess.

The noise inside the cinema is deafening. People come and go constantly, they discuss the on-screen action, boo the baddy, whistle at the lead man and everyone laughs their heads off. In the end, love wins out and we all applaud.

The protagonist is a pretty teenager from Texas who is working as a waitress to save up for the school trip of her dreams, to Paris. Her classmates – all rich, beautiful and stuck up – go to eat at the restaurant where she works.

They tease her and make fun of her, eliciting well-deserved boos from the audience. When the group arrives in Paris, the paparazzi mistake the Texan waitress for an English princess and set off in hot pursuit. The princess's servants – similarly confused by the girl's resemblance to their mistress – hustle the Texan into a limousine and sweep her off to the hotel. The original princess disappears (I can't remember why) and the waitress assumes her identity for a few days, wearing her fabulous dresses, her shoes and her jewellery. She is taken to Monaco, attends balls where everyone adores her, and even has a romance with an aristocratic young polo player. (Most of the spectators whistle with delight but some of the men jeer, presumably out of jealousy.) In the end, the deception is found out. They discover that the girl is not a princess at all but a vulgar, Texan waitress, and she packs her bags, flees Monaco and goes off to look after orphans in Romania. Just when things are looking bleak, the polo player appears, smiles at the girl and she smiles back. The End. The audience cheers.

Slightly dazed, we stagger out into the street.

'That was so funny!' Lorena says.

'No one will ever mistake me for a princess,' Rosa cackles.

They ask me if I've ever been to Paris and whether it's really like that, with that huge tower, the hotels, the palaces.

Alicia decides we should eat at Fanny's, a restaurant that serves fried chicken, hamburgers and ice creams. A large TV shows cartoons, and there's a kids' play area, fluorescent lighting and salsa music. The seven of us sit down, order chicken with fries and Coca-Cola, and continue talking about the film, speculating about what happened after the final smiles. Did they go back to Monaco together? Or to America? Perhaps they got married. Alicia says maybe they both stayed in Romania to look after the children.

For dessert we order ice cream. Evelyn wants a *payasito*, a little clown: two scoops of ice cream for the body, a cone for a hat, two wafers as the arms, and chocolate buttons for the eyes, nose and mouth. As it melts, the smiling little clown gradually sinks into the glass with its arms in the air, and Evelyn laughs with delight. Alicia has ordered an *osito*, a little bear. When she starts to eat its arms, she giggles and says it reminds her of the time she ate a chocolate bunny.

'I never told anyone before,' she says.

Last year, Alicia visited La Paz to attend the national congress of child workers. She went as a delegate of the children of Potosí – shoeshine kids, domestic workers, construction labourers, miners – aged between ten and seventeen, who held an assembly and chose eight representatives to send to the capital. They spent a week meeting with children from all over Bolivia and they also did some sightseeing.

'We slept in a barracks. We were woken up by bugles at five o'clock every morning.'

The child workers held a meeting at the Bolivian parliament and went to a reception held by President Evo

Morales, who sold ice creams in the street when he was five years old, was a llama herder at eight, and a brickmaker at twelve.

'The *cambas* talked a lot,' says Alicia. (The *cambas* are what people from the high plateau call the inhabitants of Bolivia's Amazonian lowlands.) 'They said they didn't want to work in the sugar fields.'

'And what about you?'

'Yes, I went out and spoke into the mic.'

'What did you say to Evo?'

'That the government should give us study grants. And that they have to give us water and electricity up on the Cerro.'

'And what did Evo say?'

'He said yes. And afterwards he came over to shake our hands.'

The trip to La Paz coincided with Easter, and Alicia decided to give herself a treat.

'They were selling chocolate bunnies in the street. I bought a little one.' She separates her thumb and forefinger slightly to indicate its size. 'It cost eighty cents. I ate it. Then, with the money I had left, I bought another one for my mum and my sister.'

Her mum and her sister look at her in surprise. This is the first time they have heard about the chocolate bunny.

'It was big!' She spreads her hands like a fisherman, until they are about thirty centimetres apart, and looks fondly at the invisible chocolate rabbit. 'I took it on the bus with me because I didn't want it to get broken in my holdall. But the journey was really long and I got hungry. I nibbled the tail. I told myself, "I'm just going to eat the tail. Nobody will know."'

She begins to laugh.

'Then I ate its ears ...'

The rest of them start to laugh too.

'Then the feet, then its little body ... And then I ate it all!'

By now, everyone is laughing.

'Poor little rabbit!' says Evelyn's aunt.

'Poor us!' says her mum.

* * *

Alicia presented Evo Morales with a letter from the child workers of Potosí. 'We all suffer from discrimination, exploitation and abuse because we are child and adolescent workers. We are paid less, we don't have contracts or medical insurance. People insult us and look down on us. We don't have time to study because we have to work to support our families. The authorities don't listen to us. There are laws but nobody defends our rights.'

On 18 December 2013, the police fired teargas at a children's demonstration outside the Bolivian parliament in La Paz. Thirty of the demonstrators required medical treatment. They were members of UNATSBO (Union of Child and Adolescent Workers of Bolivia) and were protesting against the Minors' Code, which proposed banning those under the age of fourteen from working.

In the face of opposition from the International Labour Organization, UNICEF and Save the Children, who all view child labour as a crime, the demonstrators convinced Bolivia's parliament to change its mind.

It was the end of a long process which could be traced back to 2007, when children demonstrated outside the parliament because the recently elected president, Evo Morales, had proposed a new constitution, including an article prohibiting 'child labour of any kind'. The children's spokespeople argued that many of them would go hungry if they weren't allowed to work, and that child labour should be regulated rather than banned, to protect children from abuse, ensure they were paid fairly and guarantee their employment rights. They won the support of several ministers and high-ranking members of the government and eventually Article 61 of the new constitution was amended to read, 'Child exploitation and forced labour are forbidden'. No particular protection is offered to minors; the forced labour and exploitation of adults are also illegal. In 2014, the parliament passed Act 548, the Children's and Adolescents' Code, which allows children over the age of ten to be self-employed and enables those over the age of twelve to work as employees, with the permission of their parents. The Code states that minors may not work in jobs that interfere with their education, jobs which are hazardous, endanger their health or hinder their personal development. It also says that the state will develop a programme to support families in extreme poverty so that minors will not be forced to work.

According to the United Nations Population Fund, there are 850,000 workers between the ages of five and seventeen in Bolivia (almost a tenth of the population). Of these, 300,000 work permanently, half of them in the very worst settings, performing some of the jobs that the Code expressly prohibits. Such as mining.

* * *

Alicia is reading a cheap paperback, a title that has been on sale for almost forty years in newsagents and book-shops across Bolivia, often in pirated editions.

The miner is doubly exploited. Firstly, his low wages mean his wife has to work far harder in the home. And it is not only his wife who is exploited but also his children. There is so much to do that sometimes we have to send our *wawas*, our kids, out to work. They have to wait in line for food, and they get shoved and crushed. When there's no meat in the shops people become so desperate that kids sometimes die just trying to get a piece of meat. It's desperate. I've heard of kids with fractured ribs, even being trampled to death. Lots of them. If they're waiting for meat for two or three days and it doesn't come, they have to queue up all day. So they miss school for two or three days. My husband works, I work, I make my kids work, so there's a whole load of us working to support the household. The woman, even if she's at home, is still caught in the system that exploits her husband. And the kids too. The bosses get richer and richer, and the situation of the workers gets worse and worse.

The book, called *Si me permiten hablar* (Let me speak), was written in 1977 by sociologist Moema Viezzer, and contains the testimony of Domitila Barrios, a miner's wife who was active in the fierce struggles of the 1960s and 1970s in Siglo XX.

'Despite everything we do, people still think women don't work because we don't make a financial contribution to the household. That it's only the man who works because he receives a wage.'

Domitila would get up at four in the morning, make breakfast for her husband, fry the huge batch of *salteñas* that her children had helped her to prepare the evening before, get the children ready for school, go out to sell the *salteñas*, spend the afternoon queuing to buy meat, vegetables and oil in the company stores – the only shops where the miners' families could spend their wages – buy wool to knit with, do the laundry by hand, help her kids with their homework and attend the meetings of the Housewives' Committee. 'I sleep four or five hours. I'm used to it.'

One day, she decided to calculate how much it would cost to pay a washerwoman, a cook, a babysitter and a cleaner to do her work.

The money needed to pay for all the work we do in the home is much more than our husbands earn in the mine [...] That's why it's so important for revolutionaries to win the first battle, in our own homes. The first battle is to allow women, men and children to take part in the struggles of the working class [...] That's why it's so important to reject this bourgeois idea that women should stay at home and not get involved in trade unions and politics. Because, even if the woman stays at home, she's still oppressed by the system that exploits her husband who works in a mine or a factory.

* * *

A young man, about twenty years old, wearing jeans, a hooded sweatshirt and running shoes, visits the hut. It's Álvaro, Alicia's older brother, who emigrated to Porco to work as a labourer but came back to Potosí because mining pays better. Now he has enough money to rent a flat in town, which he shares with other young miners, and every now and then he comes to visit his mother and his two younger sisters up on the Cerro.

He's surprised to see me here with Alicia and Rosa. We say hello, introduce ourselves and shake hands. I don't know if Alicia or Rosa have told him anything about me. He goes straight into the hut.

'Sometimes he mistreats me,' says Rosa quietly. 'He's violent. He suffered a lot because his dad beat him. When his dad died, he left school and went down the mine. It wasn't long before he started drinking.'

Álvaro was fourteen when he began working in the mine. Other kids pushed trucks, crushed the ore or even helped the drillers who work at the face, deafened by the noise and choked by the dust. Álvaro was small and agile so they sent him down the wormholes, the ones that were too small for the adult miners. It's one of the jobs that kids perform in the mines. They stick their heads in a hole at ground level, squeeze their shoulders through, press themselves flat against the rock and crawl on their bellies. They work with a hammer and a wedge. In the holes, the temperature can reach fifty degrees or more and there's no ventilation. The body of an adolescent occupies almost all the space, so there's just enough air to hold the wedge against the rock, strike it with the hammer to dislodge a few chunks of rock and see whether there's a promising seam that's worth dynamiting. Then they have to turn around if there's enough space, or crawl backwards through the hole, back to their companions – and to the air.

Álvaro is twenty years old now, and he's too big for the wormholes. He does other jobs, shovelling rock or pushing trucks. He earns enough to pay the rent on a flat, and he comes to visit from time to time. For example, when he has clothes to be washed.

He comes out of the hut after spending some time with Evelyn, and nods at Alicia. She goes over and takes a tracksuit, a couple of tee-shirts and some underpants from the clothes line. His laundry, which Rosa did earlier. Alicia folds it up, puts it in a bag and hands it to Álvaro. He kisses his mother on the cheek, mutters a goodbye, and leaves.

* * *

Among the stories that Domitila Barrios tells, there is one that makes a particularly strong impression on Alicia. It took place during the dictatorship of General Barrientos. The soldiers arrested Domitila in Siglo XX, accused her of being a communist guerrilla and locked her up. She was eight months pregnant. They interrogated her, kicked and punched her, bloodied her face and knocked out six of her teeth. One of the soldiers pinned her to the ground and kneeled on her belly with all his weight until she could hardly breathe. They showed her a knife and told her they were going to use it to chop up her baby. In the cell, Domitila went into labour. 'I told myself, I don't want my child to be born alive. I don't want the colonel to murder my child. The head was ready to come out but I pushed it back in.' Domitila gave birth. She lost consciousness. And when she woke up she saw the baby lying in a puddle in the middle of the floor: cold, purple and dead.

Among the stories Domitila Barrios tells, there is one that particularly amuses Alicia. The miners of Siglo XX and their wives marched all the way to La Paz to protest because the company owed them several months' wages. When they reached the city, the army arrested the leaders. So the women occupied a building and went on hunger strike. Within a few hours, Claudio San Román – the notorious head of the Office of Political Control, a torturer with a terrifying reputation – arrived. He entered the building with his soldiers and a small woman wearing a bowler hat, a woollen jacket and peasant's skirts came running towards him. 'We don't have any guns,' the woman shouted, 'but we'll blast everything to hell right now, because we're carrying dynamite and we'd rather be blown up than be tortured by the likes of you!'

San Román knew this was a timeworn tactic. The women from Siglo XX tied dynamite to their bodies when the army entered the camp to arrest the miners, and they even attached explosives to their children. The little woman showed San Román a bulge under her jacket and hurried back towards her companions, shouting, 'Quick, quick. Give me a light! I'm going to blow myself up right now.' San Román and his men scarpered. Then the woman sat down, trembling with nerves, opened her jacket and showed the bulge to her comrades: it was her baby's bottle.

* * *

The women's hunger strike took place in 1961 and spread right across the country, with groups of workers and students joining in. The government gave in after ten days. It freed the miners, paid them the wages they were owed, and resupplied the shops and hospitals in the mining camps, which were controlled by the state at that time. The women went back to Llallagua in a blaze of glory, ready to continue with their political struggles, and founded the Siglo XX Housewives' Committee. Sixty women joined. They marched triumphantly around the camp and then several of them joined the miners' leaders on the balcony of the trade union building to give speeches.

'You should have heard the men laughing when they saw us!' Domitila Barrios recalled. 'They said, "The women have organized a front! Let them! It won't last two days, they'll make a front against each other and that'll be the end of it." They weren't used to listening to women. When the women tried to speak from the balcony, the men shouted, "Go home! Do your cooking! Do your laundry!" And they whistled and laughed.'

3

The Powder Keg

Gregorio Iriarte was posted to Siglo XX in early 1964, just when the powder keg was about to blow.

'I'll never forget the first time I saw the radio building. It was guarded by men with rifles and sticks of dynamite. Tensions were running high between the radio station of the communist trade union, the Miner's Voice, and the Church's Radio Pius XII, which I'd been sent to run. It was the Cold War, pure and simple, East against West, communism against capitalism, one radio station against another. With bullets and dynamite. Just remembering it makes me ashamed.'

Father Gregorio Iriarte smiles and narrows his eyes. He talks calmly and at length. He is eighty-six years old, has very fine white hair, and his small lively eyes flick to and fro behind thick glasses. He laughs frequently as he recounts his life with a certain sense of wonder, as if slightly embarrassed or astonished by the terrible events he has witnessed, as if he needs to distance himself from them in some way.

'The truth is, they moved me to Llallagua like a pawn on the Cold War chessboard. The way the Church saw it, Latin America was threatened by the spread of communism. And the most communist place on the whole continent was Siglo XX in Llallagua. So in 1959 the Church set up Radio Pius XII, manned by a group of Canadian priests – the Oblate Fathers – to combat the communist message. I was sent there in 1964 to replace the director because things weren't going too well.'

The relationship between the priests and the miners was extremely tense. At a time when the Bolivian government was arresting and exiling communist miners' leaders, the Oblates railed against communism over the airwaves.

The government was controlled by the Movimiento Nacional Revolucionario, which had won the general election of 1951 and, the following year, instigated a revolution. The new president, Paz Estenssoro, introduced universal suffrage for the first time in Bolivia's history; until then, it had been restricted by sex, education and income, so that only a few privileged men (2.5 per cent of the total population) were entitled to vote. He repealed racist laws such as those forbidding Quechua and Aymara people from entering the main squares in many towns and cities. He outlawed *pongueaje*, the feudal servitude that landowners imposed on indigenous families. He reformed landownership, expropriating the large estates that constituted 95 per cent of the country's agricultural land, and redistributing them among the peasantry. And he introduced free, compulsory education and created a universal social security system.

And he nationalized the mines. The ore deposits and processing facilities of the mining barons – Aramayo, Hochschild and Patiño (who had died a year earlier) – passed into the hands of the state, under the control of a new public enterprise: Comibol, the Mining Corporation of Bolivia. The wealth generated by tin would finally serve to develop Bolivia. That was the plan.

But Comibol was a disaster.

Things didn't start too badly. When it was created in 1952, Comibol was the world's second-largest producer of tin. At the beginning, it made money and the state improved the conditions of its workers: wages went up; employment rights were recognized; health, hygiene, housing, food and education in the camps all improved.

But Comibol soon became a bureaucratic monster and a political machine. The trade unions took part in decision-making – they called it workers' control – and the trade union leaders became bosses. They found positions for their allies, created jobs for their supporters and wove a dense web of patronage. In just five years Comibol's workforce grew from 24,000 to 35,600, only one in three of whom were miners. The rest had office jobs in the company's bureaucracy. 'It had the least efficient workforce and the highest labour costs of any mining company in the world,' writes engineer Jorge Espinoza. The waste of public money was scandalous. Directors spent cash on parties, banquets and holidays, made donations and awarded grants, and paid vastly inflated prices to suppliers who also happened to be personal friends.

To make matters worse, the deposits that had been worked by the tin barons for nearly half a century were beginning to run out. Comibol failed to invest in prospecting, didn't open any new mines and didn't modernize its obsolete technology because all the company's money was being siphoned off by placemen. The trade unions fought against the government – and amongst themselves – with shows of strength that inevitably involved strikes. In an average year, between thirty and forty days were lost to stoppages in the mines, and in the worst years the total could be far higher: in 1961, no fewer than 210 days were lost to industrial action, and in 1963 the figure was only slightly lower, at 195. Comibol's costs rocketed while annual output plummeted from 25,000 tons of tin to just 12,000. Bolivia's mining sector haemorrhaged millions of dollars every year.

The vast enterprise was also a tool through which the state exercised political control. Low wages were supplemented by a network of services – housing, education, health, subsidized food in the company stores – which ensured the dependency of the miners. By filling or emptying the shelves, raising or lowering prices, allocating housing, the state could reward or punish the miners at times of strike or unrest.

The revolution gradually disintegrated. Bolivia was completely dependent on tin exports, and when prices crashed there was no money to pay for public education and social security or to fund the operation of the mines. There was, in other words, no money to pay for the revolution.

The collapse in the price of tin was no accident. It was the result of a decision taken by the United States.

This is how it played out. During the Second World War, the mining oligarchs sold 173,000 tons of tin to the United States at rock-bottom prices, well below the official rate, as an act of friendship during wartime. The United States built up reserves of 350,000 tons, the equivalent of two years' worth of global tin output. And Bolivia received 670 million dollars less than it would have been paid had it sold the ore at market prices. Six hundred and seventy million dollars.

When the revolutionary party won the elections and came to power, the United States took umbrage and implemented three measures designed to suffocate Bolivia: they blocked Bolivia's exports, depriving it of income; they demanded that the country repay foreign debt of 62 million dollars, a debt that had been frozen in 1931 and whose repayment the United States had never demanded while the mining oligarchs were in control; and they flooded the global tin market by selling off 50,000 tons of their stockpile. In other words, they sold off the tin that Bolivia had given them almost for nothing, the bottom fell out of the market and Bolivia was ruined.

With the country on the verge of starvation, President Paz Estenssoro accepted the conditions imposed by the United States and the International Monetary Fund. Bolivia – with a population of just three million – became the largest recipient of North American money, with Washington supporting one third of the national budget. But the cash came with strings attached. Paz Estenssoro signed contracts with North American companies to operate Bolivia's oilfields; he paid out the huge sums that Patiño's heirs were demanding as compensation for the nationalization of the mines; and he reshaped his own government on instructions from the US State Department, got rid of those ministers with links to the trade union and communist movements, and eliminated workers' control in Comibol.

The left-wing groups that had supported the government – Marxists, Trotskyists, trade unionists, student movements – organized strikes and demonstrations against Paz Estenssoro. The new vice-president, General Barrientos, was in the pay of the CIA and at the time of his appointment in August 1964 was already plotting the military coup that would bring him to power just three months later.

* * *

That was when Gregorio Iriarte arrived to take charge of the Catholic radio station in Siglo XX. When the powder keg was about to blow.

The Oblate Fathers railed against the practices of the Bolivian miners, who held processions with statues of saints and the Virgin Mary but also incorporated devil dances, Andean spirits and revelry into their festivities. The dramatic clash of cultures was exacerbated by ideological differences. In 1961 the miners accused the priests of collaborating with the army, identifying trade union leaders who were then arrested and sent into internal exile in the Amazon region. The miners surrounded the radio station, hurled dynamite at the building and paraded a figure dressed in a cassock, with a placard round his neck which read 'Foreign priests go home!' They marched to the church, sang the *Internationale* and burned the effigy.

In Llallagua, everyone listened to Claudio Marañón, the anarchist commentator who had a regular slot on the Miner's Voice. He didn't mince his words, describing the priests as 'wolves in sheep's clothing', 'agents in the service of North American imperialism, distributing Yankee alms to the peasantry', 'vampires' and 'enemies of the Bolivian working class'. He denounced one of the Canadian priests, Father Mauricio Lefebvre, arguing that Lefebvre was not even a real Christian because 'he wants humanity – that same humanity for which Jesus of Nazareth suffered on the cross on Calvary – to be imprisoned, deceived and exploited by vicious slave drivers, cruel capitalists and the bloodthirsty arms dealers of the American dollar'.

One morning, a Radio Pius XII employee was sent out to buy supplies for the priests. He ran over a dog and it just so happened that the animal belonged to Marañón. The next news bulletin, read by Marañón himself, led with the headline 'Imperialist truck runs over proletarian dog!'

'The Llallagua union was the most powerful in the country,' says Gregorio Iriarte. 'If it went on strike, tin exports were halted. And the government found itself in dire straits because it had no foreign currency and couldn't pay for anything. The government sent the army in to arrest the leaders and shoot at the demonstrators. There was no messing around in Llallagua.'

During his first two weeks in the camp, Iriarte visited the miners' families in their homes.

'I immediately realized how terribly exploited they were. My God, what living conditions!'

The miners lived in the old Patiño camp. The houses were small and in terrible condition. Each accommodated a miner, his wife and their children, and if the miner had a brother or a cousin, then he might live there too with his family, so that ten, twelve or fifteen people would be crammed into a two-room dwelling. There was no heating or running water and no toilets, just communal latrines. The only doctors in Siglo XX were there to treat the engineers and managers, who lived in elegant villas outside the camp. The women did their shopping at the company store, queuing for hours because deliveries were erratic and unpredictable. If they were told that meat, eggs or oil were due to arrive the next day, the women and their children would queue through the night to avoid going home empty-handed.

'And then there was the work in the mine. They died like flies.'

Many of them were killed by rockfalls, fell down a shaft or were caught in a dynamite explosion. Worst of all was the silicosis. After just a few years, a miner's lungs began to rot and he couldn't breathe. The company threw the miner out of his job, threw the family out of its home, and threw the kids out of school. The family's only solution was to return to the village in search of shelter or to beg for money in the street.

'So many miners were reduced to begging!'

* * *

'The road out of Siglo XX is lined by a great mass of humanity,' wrote René Poppe, philosopher and former miner.

There are the blind and the mutilated, those who have lost a hand or a foot or have been crippled in some other way. They have not come here from elsewhere. They come from the mine. And they pray for the souls of the dead.

Unfit for work in the mine, they can't go back to their villages and all that is left to them is to pray for the dead. People here are generous. They scarcely have enough to eat, but they share what little they have. They give the blind and the crippled a coin and ask them to say a prayer for the dead.

'The problem in Llallagua wasn't communism, it was injustice,' says Iriarte.

He lives in the residence for retired Oblate Fathers in Cochabamba. The walls of his room are almost completely bare, adorned only by a small crucifix and a poster for the Charlie Chaplin movie *The Kid*, in which the Tramp leads an abandoned child by the hand. The only other items in the room are a bed, a wardrobe and a desk with books and papers, at which he sits and writes. He has just finished the seventeenth edition of his best-known work, the monumental *Análisis crítico de la realidad*, a critical analysis of reality. He published it in 1983 and has updated it constantly ever since. The book is 700 pages long and provides a detailed analysis of wealth and poverty, of inequality, development, health and educa- tion, of the problems of childhood, narco-trafficking, ecology, human rights, globalization, the media and a host of other issues – in Bolivia, in Latin America, in the world. It can be found in bookshops and classrooms. And on the bookshelves of several Bolivian presidents. Evo Morales kept a copy beside his bed when he was running for the presidency, and asked Iriarte to explain its contents to him.

Iriarte was born in Olazagutía in northern Spain. His father worked in a cement factory and was a member of every association in the village, and his mother was a housewife who gave Iriarte a single piece of advice when he was ordained: 'Never abandon the poor'.

Iriarte presents me with two of his books and then takes me to the visitors' room, which has a sofa, some armchairs and a table with two glasses of water.

I began to wonder if it wasn't all a terrible injustice, if perhaps Radio Pius XII was wrong to always take the side of the company and the government. One day, I met Federico Escóbar. He was the leader of the miners' union, a no-nonsense man, tough, well respected. I'd only been in Llallagua for a few days when some of the trade unionists came to ask me to bless their new projector. The union had a cinema in Siglo XX. I say it was a cinema, but it was just a bare room, really, with a few chairs. I didn't want to go, I didn't trust them, but they insisted and in the end I went along. I entered the room and there were several union men there. One of them was Escóbar. We greeted each other very politely and the men removed their hats, as if they were waiting for me to say the blessing. I didn't know how to start, what to say. Sitting on top of the projector were three bottles of beer. So I said, 'You can open the beer because there isn't going to be any holy water here.' Escóbar replied, 'If there's no holy water, then there's no beer either.' I didn't say anything. Then he said, 'Father, you don't want to bless the projector because you think we're going to use it to show communist films. Well, good things, holy things, don't need to be blessed. If you think we're going to use this for something bad, then you've got to bless it.' I laughed. In the end I blessed the projector, we drank the beer and Escóbar said something that made a big impression on me. 'You won't understand this,' he told me, 'but I'm one hundred per cent communist and one hundred per cent Catholic. I fight against injustice and against exploitation.' Well, me too! 'You've seen how the miners live,' he went on. 'So tell me, is Radio Pius XII going to be with them or is it going to carry on supporting the company? If you're with the miners, then I'll be at your side. But if you're with the company, then I'll be against you. Just ask yourself one question. If Christ was here – and he's your model and mine – then which side would he be on? Don't you think he'd be with the poor and the victims of injustice?' It really affected me and I went home and said to the other Oblate Fathers, 'I think we're making a mistake. There are three or four real communists at most, the others follow them because they're fighting against injustice. And we should do the same. We have to be on the side of the poor and the persecuted. It's not a political question, it's a human question, a religious question.'

Iriarte sips some water and smiles sheepishly.

Hard times were coming. In November 1964, General Barrientos launched a *coup d'état* and one of his first measures was to cut the miners' wages in half. Every mine in the country went on strike and the army responded with massive repression: they occupied the mines, fired on the miners and arrested their leaders. Before long, the mines were working again. All except for Siglo XX. The army had surrounded the camp but they didn't dare enter because it was heavily defended and fierce fighting would be inevitable.

The army sent a message for the Oblate Fathers to read out over the radio. 'If Federico Escóbar does not surrender, we will search the camp until we find him.'

The communist Escóbar went to Iriarte's house to ask for advice.

'I proposed an escape plan,' Iriarte says. 'Otherwise, they were going to kill him!'

They met at five o'clock the next morning, before dawn. They wanted to leave the camp under cover of darkness. There were three of them: a young Canadian who worked with the Oblate Fathers and who would drive the car; Father Iriarte, in a cassock that he never normally wore but which he hoped would impress the soldiers; and Federico Escóbar, in a jacket and tie and with a false identity document prepared by the priests, in the name of Francisco Belzu, a Llallagua businessman.

Before getting into the car, Escóbar asked Iriarte to do something.

'Father. Let's say three Hail Marys, to protect us on the journey.'

Iriarte laughed. 'But Federico, don't Marxists say that fear is what creates gods?'

'Maybe, but I promise you I pray every night without fear.'

They said their Hail Marys and got into the car. Iriarte had a packet of cigarettes in his pocket. He didn't smoke but he thought it might be good to offer them to the soldiers and help take some of the tension out of the situation. When they reached the military roadblock it was still dark. A captain saluted Iriarte. The priest smiled, got out of the car and shook the officer's hand.

'Father, I'm going to ask for your cooperation,' the captain said. 'We need to arrest some subversives but we know the miners are waiting for us and they're armed. Please tell us how they've organized. And where the leaders are. I'm going to call the colonel so you can explain.'

'Captain, how could you think of waking the colonel up at this time of night? I'll tell you what. I'm on my way to Oruro to say mass, and I promised to give Mr Belzu a lift because he has some business in town. When I get back, we can talk at our leisure and I'll give you whatever help I can.'

The captain agreed, but asked them to show him their documents because he had to register all comings and goings from the camp. Iriarte handed over the three documents and the captain started to read them by the light of the car headlamps. He examined Iriarte's document first, then the Canadian's, and when he was about to inspect Escóbar's fake identification card, Iriarte offered him the cigarettes.

'Here, Captain. Share these out among your men. They must have had a long night.'

The captain took the cigarettes, thanked Iriarte, returned the documents without paying any more attention to them, and lifted the barrier.

Iriarte left Escóbar in Oruro, where his party comrades were waiting for him in another vehicle to take him through the desert and across the border to Chile. When Iriarte and the driver returned to Llallagua, the commander invited the priest into his office and asked him about the miners' organization, what steps they were taking, what positions they had fortified. Iriarte told him that nothing was going on, the miners weren't armed, there was no need for violence. The commander laughed.

'*Ay*, Father! You priests are all so gullible.'

Iriarte gives a sly smile as he recalls it.

'A few months later, they arrested Escóbar as he was trying to re-enter Bolivia from Brazil using the same false papers. They must have made him talk, because that document caused me a load of trouble.'

Some weeks later, Iriarte received a call from President Barrientos, who wanted to have a quiet chat about the situation in Siglo XX and invited Iriarte to lunch at the presidential palace in La Paz.

I went to see him a few days later. They set a small table for us in the courtyard, just the two of us. That's how he was: very chatty, very personable. We talked about all sorts of things, the miners, the radio station, it was all quite amicable. Then suddenly he said, 'Father, who took Escóbar to Chile?' 'I did.' 'I thought as much. Did you also obtain the fake document?' 'Yes.' 'You know that's a crime, don't you?' 'Yes, Mr President, but saving somebody's life is more important than falsifying a document.' I told him that Escóbar was a good person, that he hadn't committed any crimes, that he worked for the miners' rights, that the miners had lots of problems, as both of us well knew. Barrientos nodded and said he understood. 'But as you can imagine, Father, the army were furious. They're angry with me and they want me to do something.'

Barrientos did something. He showed up at Siglo XX, stood on a platform in the main square, and delivered a speech in Spanish and Quechua. He told the miners that he had slashed their wages in half because Comibol had been bankrupted by the corruption of the revolutionary government, that he had reduced their pay to avoid laying off the company's 35,000 employees, that the cut would only last for one year, that he would sort out Comibol's finances and then give them back the money they had lost, that he would share the profits with them, that their sacrifice would be rewarded.

A few weeks later he sent soldiers with machine guns into Siglo XX. He had outlawed the trade unions, deported

300 union organizers to the Amazon jungle and wanted to arrest the last of the union leaders, who were hiding in the mines. As part of Barrientos' operation, the army invaded the camp, occupied the settlement street by street and house by house, and strafed the panicking crowds from the air: eighty-two people were killed and more than 200 were injured.

'On Radio Pius XII we denounced the massacre, and the army wasn't happy with us,' Iriarte says. 'One night, they fired two mortars at the building. It woke up the whole camp. A huge crowd came to the radio station. By then, the miners supported us, they could see that we were on their side and the army was attacking the priests to silence us. The army barracks were very close by but nobody came to ask about the bombs. Everybody knew it had been them.'

The 'red' massacre – attacks, shooting, machine guns – was followed by a 'white' massacre: Comibol dismissed hundreds of miners who were linked to the trade unions, evicted their families from their homes and expelled their children from school.

* * *

Following the massacre, Barrientos received a million dollars from the CIA to fund his campaign in the election he called in 1966 to lend legitimacy to his presidency, two years after he had taken power by force. His main rivals were disqualified from running, and after an easy victory Barrientos got down to the business of signing agreements: establishing an American military base at El Alto; granting concessions to US mining firm Philips; and enabling Gulf Oil to conduct operations with the Bolivian state oil company, YPFB, on terms that were extraordinarily generous to the Americans. Just in case anyone protested, the minister of the interior was another CIA man, Antonio Arguedas: many years later, he would confirm that US agents participated in the interrogation, disappearance and murder of union leaders.

Barrientos' star signing, however, was a shady wheeler-dealer called Klaus Altmann, a German gentleman with Bolivian nationality. He was put in charge of the equally dubious state shipping company, Transmarítima: it only had one vessel – a riverboat – and its official activities were minimal.

Klaus Altmann was a Nazi fugitive whose real name was Klaus Barbie. As head of the Gestapo in Lyon during the Second World War, he had ordered the assassination of 4,432 people, overseen the torture of 14,311 more and sent around 7,500 to the death camps. He liked taking personal responsibility for his work. He tortured men, women and children himself, breaking their arms and legs, applying electric shocks, raping them, flaying them, setting dogs on them, drowning them in buckets of ammonia. After the war, Barbie ditched his old identity, fled to Bolivia and adopted a new surname. Altmann had been the name of the rabbi in his home town. Barbie offered his services to

Barrientos, and the offer was received enthusiastically. The riverboat company served as a cover for arms trafficking, undercover funding of the regime and the assassination of dissidents. According to Amnesty International, the death squads organized by Barbie murdered between 3,000 and 8,000 of the government's opponents.

* * *

Among the many thousands of deaths was one of which Klaus Barbie was particularly proud: the death of Adolfo Mena González, a Uruguayan businessman who entered Bolivia in November 1966 and was also operating under a false name and profession. Adolfo Mena was Che Guevara.

In April 1967, Che's supporters released a message that he had written before leaving Cuba for Bolivia. It began with a quote from the nineteenth-century Cuban revolutionary José Martí: 'Now is the time of furnaces but we must look to the light'. The message went on to reject the unjust peace of the post-war period and called for a global conflict, a 'long and cruel war' that would lead to 'the total destruction of imperialism' and establish a more just world order. This battle would require the use of 'hatred as an element of the struggle; a relentless hatred of the enemy, impelling us over and beyond the natural limitations to which man is heir, and transforming him into an effective, violent, selective and cold killing machine. That is how our soldiers must be; a people without hatred cannot vanquish a brutal enemy.' Che argued that the future would be bright if only the forces of revolution could manage to ignite 'two, three or many Vietnams throughout the world, with their share of deaths and their immense tragedies, their everyday heroism and their repeated blows against imperialism, impelled to disperse its forces under the sudden attack and the increasing hatred of all peoples of the world!'

In the remote mountains of Ñancahuazú he organized a band of fifty guerrilla fighters, almost all Bolivians or Cubans, and there he repeated his message. 'Bolivia must be sacrificed so that the revolutions in neighbouring countries may begin. We must create a new Vietnam in the Americas, with its centre in Bolivia.' Che predicted that a Bolivian war would spread to the country's neighbours, forcing the United States to intervene in South America and thus dragging the Soviet Union and China into war against the USA. In a remote camp in the Bolivian mountains, Che was convinced that his guerrillas were about to light the fuse that would start the Third World War. He also assigned to Bolivia the same fate allocated to it by so many others over the previous 500 years: to be sacrificed.

* * *

One day Che's forces issued a communiqué, and the signatories included several miners from Siglo XX. At the same time, the leaders of the banned miners' union announced that all workers would donate a *mita* – one day's wages – to the guerrillas.

'That was reckless,' says Iriarte.

Barrientos had declared a state of emergency and the army was looking for an excuse to invade the camp again.

'None of us thought the danger was that great, but the CIA and the Bolivian army had a very clear strategy: to attack the guerrilla vanguard but also to strike the rearguard in the mines. They planned an assault on Siglo XX. And they deliberately sought to provoke a massacre, to teach the miners a lesson.'

The army chose the winter solstice, an important festival in Bolivia. The miners and their families spent the night celebrating, lighting bonfires, roasting meat in the street, singing and drinking.

The army didn't arrive by road, as they had on previous occasions. They wanted the benefit of surprise. At four in the morning a train full of soldiers arrived at Cancañiri, an ore-loading station a little higher up the mountain. The soldiers were fired up. Before such operations the officers handed out bottles of brandy, encouraged their men to drink, harangued them, and then unleashed them like wild beasts.

At 4.20, the miners were sleeping off their revelry in the streets of the camp.

Some of the bonfires were still burning.

The soldiers came down the mountain, yelling like banshees and unleashing bursts of machine-gun fire into the darkness. They ran through the streets, firing at random, pursuing people into their homes, kicking down the doors and shooting anyone they caught. They gunned down drunk men, children, old women – anyone in their path. They forced their way into the communal latrines and shot the occupants.

'I remember a girl who appeared at the radio station in tears,' says Iriarte. 'She'd just come out of the toilet and a bullet had passed through her dress. It was a miracle she was still alive. And I remember Fidelia. She lived near the station. She was pregnant. She'd got up to make breakfast on the remains of one of the bonfires and she was hit by a mortar. It destroyed her, ripping her stomach open. Her baby stuck out a hand, it was being born and was dying right there on the embers, burnt, next to its mother's dead body.'

The next day, Iriarte went to the morgue and counted twenty-six corpses.

'Apart from García Maisman, a communist leader who had gone out with a rifle to confront the soldiers, all the others were workers, nightwatchmen, women who had gone out to use the toilet or make breakfast. And children. I'll always remember the number: twenty-six, just like the twenty-six Americans who were in charge of Comibol. They organized everything with the army. And there's no doubt there were more deaths, lots more. Nobody knows how many, because lots of people fled to the mountain and disappeared. The army got them and that was the last anyone heard of them.'

The army destroyed the Miner's Voice. The priests, the only ones who still had a microphone, reported the massacre, denounced the army's brutality and pointed the finger at Barrientos. The army responded by threatening the priests.

'Either I left Llallagua or they would shut the station down,' Iriarte says. 'I had to get out.'

* * *

Che Guevara thought that the Llallagua massacre would bring the miners over to the side of the guerrilla uprising en masse. He was wrong. Throughout the course of the campaign, only a few dozen fighters had joined Che's ranks. The Bolivian communists were furious because Che had deceived them about his true intentions on his arrival in the country and because – just as in the Congo – he had not involved them in his preparations for the uprising. As a result, they distanced themselves from the guerrilla campaign and abandoned Che to his fate. Klaus Barbie and the American Green Berets organized a special force of 400 soldiers, who pursued the guerrillas through the mountains and captured Che. They took their prisoner to the village of La Higuera. That night, a helicopter arrived. On board were a Bolivian colonel and a Cuban CIA agent, who took photos and accompanied Che during the final hours of his life. The CIA agent wanted to take Che to Panama for interrogation, but the next morning the Bolivian officers received a direct order from President Barrientos that Che was to be killed. The task was entrusted to Sergeant Mario Terán, who had lost three comrades in the final battle against the guerrillas. Terán raked Che's body with machine-gun fire to make it look as if he had died in combat.

*   *   *

'Worst of all is the dust.'

The *canchamina* is covered with small stones that fall from the trucks and which the miners don't bother to pick up. Gusts of wind whip up clouds of dust that gets into your eyes and forces you to bow your head.

'When we're not crying from sadness, we cry because of the dust,' says Rosa, half smiling.

Alicia and Rosa sweep the esplanade, pressing their brooms hard against the ground and dragging the stones into heaps. Rosa pushes her broom with long slow movements, with the age-old resignation of one who has been sentenced to sweep the whole world; Alicia pushes her broom with short rapid movements, confident that this task will soon come to an end. They sweep the stones into heaps then load them onto a tarpaulin. Rosa hoists the bundle up onto her shoulders and carries the stones to the area behind the adobe hut, where it is slightly more sheltered from the wind. She unloads the stones until they form a pyramid, a metre high. Trapped inside is the wage that she can only release by cracking open the stones.

Alicia helps her. She whacks the stones with a mallet, sweeps the worthless gravel aside with her naked hand, and every now and then picks out a nugget of ore.

'I don't want my daughter to get worn out like me.'

A gust of wind envelops Rosa and she clutches her wide-brimmed hat to protect her face. She pulls up the collar of her woollen coat to cover her chin so that only her cheeks – red and roughened by the wind, the dust and the sun – are visible. She purses her lips, which are slightly deformed at the right corner. And when the wind abates, she lifts her head again and blinks rapidly to relieve her stinging eyes. Then she shows me her hands, the fingers swollen, deformed and black.

Rosa breaks up the stones until she has a full load.

'I fill a tipper with ore and then I can sell it.'

It takes her three or four months to fill a lorry. Six tons, which will fetch about 190 dollars, depending on the purity of the mineral. Of those 190 dollars, the cooperative deducts 25 for working on its land, 25 for transport, and 25 for the health fund, leaving her with just 115 dollars every three or four months.

'But I don't have medical insurance or anything.'

The cooperative deducts the money for the contributions, she explains, but it doesn't make the payments.

'I think there are problems with the documents. They wrote down my name wrong. I'm not on the list. They take the money but I don't have any insurance.'

When her husband died from silicosis, her two oldest children moved away to find work and Rosa was left alone with the youngsters, Alicia and Evelyn. She'd like to bring her mother, Juana, to live at Cerro Rico with them. But

Juana doesn't want to come. She lives in Coroma, the family's home village: it's very high up, very cold, and the only crops that grow up there are feathergrass and, if the frosts don't get them, a few potatoes. The people survive by rearing llamas and sheep. Rosa and her husband Nicolás left the village and came to the mines in search of work.

'My mum doesn't want to come. She says we suffer too much on the Cerro. She visits once a year, for All Saints' Day, and we make altars for the spirits of our dead. She never used to come, because she hated my husband. Nicolás was bad. He beat me. He would drink, come home, push me, kick me, pull my hair. My mother hated him; that's why she never came.'

Rosa points to the deformity at the corner of her mouth.

'Nicolás did that to me.'

She pulls up the sleeve of her coat to reveal a white scar on her forearm, a couple of inches long.

That was a bite. He had a nasty temper. In the mine he earned 400 pesos a week. Just 150 he gave me, to buy food, clothes for the kids, for the house. Sometimes it ran out. And if I said anything, he'd get mad and beat me. He beat my son until he bled. That's why Álvaro turned out so mean, and now he works in the mine too, and he drinks like his father. I lost two kids from the beatings. I was six months gone with my second child, and he kicked me and punched me and the baby came out dead. After Álvaro and Alicia, I got pregnant again. Nicolás kept the money, and I didn't have enough so I had to find work. I got a job doing the foundations for the sewers. There I was, with my big belly, pregnant, working on a building site. The *wawa* came out dead. Nicolás said I'd killed it, it was my fault for working, I'd done it on purpose, and he beat me. He didn't hit Alicia, thank God, because she was still small. Or Evelyn, because he died just after she was born. But he hit my mother, that's why she hated him and didn't come to see us for so many years. He beat me in front of the children. I think that's why God took him away first. If I'd died first, I don't want to think what he would have done with my kids, what would have happened to them.

* * *

Alicia walks up the hill. She's carrying a sports bag full of her aunt Lorena's clothes, which Rosa has washed. Lorena lives a quarter of a mile away, on another *canchamina* where half a dozen huts are huddled together. They're safer that way, the guards and their families looking out for each other.

'The miners are always watching, to see if we're alone so they can steal our money or do whatever they want, because up here there's no police, nothing like that.'

When she's walking alone on the Cerro, Alicia keeps a rock in her pocket.

'The miners drink. I keep a lookout and if I see drunks then I take a different route. I carry the rock because some of them are dangerous and they attack you.'

I ask about her friends who were raped and became pregnant. She says nothing for a few seconds. Then she points to a ditch, next to the group of houses where her aunt Lorena lives.

'Another girl – a friend of mine – buried two *wawas* there.'

'What happened?'

'She was raped twice by miners. The first time, she miscarried. The second time, the *wawa* was born but she drowned it. My mum and my aunt helped her to bury the *wawas* down there.'

'How old is she?'

'She's sixteen now. I always try to go with my mum or my sister. Up here, you don't want to be alone.'

* * *

'They killed all my friends,' says Gregorio Iriarte. 'Mauricio Lefebvre, Luis Espinal, Marcelo Quiroga, Federico Escóbar. All of them. I was arrested and expelled from the country three times. I was lucky. I learned how to survive underground because the years that followed the Banzer coup were terrible, really terrible.'

After the army made him leave Llallagua, Iriarte moved to La Paz. There were seven years of coups, counter-coups, guerrilla warfare and massacres, and then came the hardest blow of all: the coup that brought Colonel Hugo Banzer to power. The colonel (soon to become a general) had been a star student at the School of the Americas, the United States academy in Panama where tens of thousands of Latin American officers were trained in 'anti-communist counter-insurgency' throughout the Cold War. The school's training manuals, which were revealed many years later, explained how to torture, assassinate and kidnap suspects, and how to blackmail and manipulate their relatives. The school's graduates provided the cohort of dictators who, during the 1970s and 1980s, implemented Operation Condor, a CIA-coordinated alliance of South American dictatorships which persecuted and disappeared thousands of political activists. Banzer applied his learning diligently; he banned political parties, dissolved the trade unions, closed the universities for a year and a half, locked up and tortured hundreds of his opponents, and disappeared 150 of them.

Iriarte led a double life. Publicly, he oversaw the Church's social programmes, setting up housing cooperatives for workers, creating radio schools, raising funds to help people living in poverty. In secret, he created the Permanent Assembly of Human Rights with Father Tumiri and helped coordinate resistance to the dictatorship. The organization publicly denounced murders and disappearances, gave press conferences in Europe and North America, launched a campaign to demand amnesty for the thousands of people whom the regime had imprisoned or deported, and called for free elections. Banzer began to feel the heat.

I think the only reason they didn't kill me was because I was very careful ... and very lucky. I knew my phone was tapped, I checked any parcels before I opened them, I slept in a different bed every night, and I always walked against the flow of the traffic so I would be able to see if anyone was coming, to give me time to run. At home, I had things ready in case I had to make a quick getaway: I knew who lived next door, if I could jump the fence, if there was a dog on the other side that might give me away. I knew how to escape without being seen, where to find people who would help me. Wherever I slept, the next morning I always left the room looking as if nobody had been there.

Iriarte received a call in December 1977. Four women were about to go on hunger strike against the dictatorship and they wanted him to act as an intermediary to enable them to hold their protest in the Archbishop's Palace in La Paz, where they thought they would be safe from the army. The women, the wives of four miners' leaders from Llallagua, were called Aurora Lora, Nelly Paniagua, Angélica Flores and Luzmila Pimentel. Their husbands were all in exile and the women survived on donations from their comrades in the camp.

They decided to go on hunger strike with their fourteen children. When a journalist asked them if they were worried about the risk of going without food, one of them replied:

'In the mines, we're always on hunger strike. It starts the day you're born.'

Iriarte arranged for the women and their children to travel secretly from the mines to the Archbishop's Palace in the centre of La Paz, a stone's throw from the government buildings where Banzer had his office. A room was made ready for them and a doctor was provided to attend to the children. Then the women called the press, announced their hunger strike and read out their demands: a general amnesty, the reinstatement of sacked miners, recognition of the unions and the withdrawal of the army from the camps. Monsignor Manrique, the Archbishop of La Paz, declared that the women were his guests and he would not permit their removal.

'The Archbishop was afraid,' says Iriarte, laughing. '"Gregorio," he said, "these women won't be carrying dynamite, will they?" I assured him that the protest would be peaceful. Our aim was to have groups on hunger strike all over the country, to put Banzer under a lot of pressure.'

Three days later, a group of eleven protesters went on hunger strike in the offices of *Presencia*, a newspaper published by the Catholic Church. Among them were Domitila Barrios, two Catalan Jesuits and human rights activists – Luis Espinal and Xavier Albó – and representatives of the universities, the theatre, and women's associations. Over the following weeks, more groups installed themselves in churches, schools, universities, newspaper offices and mines the length and breadth of Bolivia. Within three weeks, more than 1,200 people were on hunger strike. Silent demonstrations were held in a number of cities.

At dawn on 17 January 1978, the police forced their way into the building. Iriarte was alerted and arrived in time to see fifty armed policemen dragging out the strikers, who were exhausted after eighteen days without food. Following some heated exchanges, the strikers agreed to leave without resistance, but asked that Huáscar Cajías, the newspaper's editor, be allowed to recite the Beatitudes:

'Blessed are those who are persecuted for the sake of righteousness ...'

The policemen, Iriarte recalls, lowered their gaze.

There were more armed attacks on strikers at the university and in churches. Monsignor Manrique threatened to place the city of La Paz under interdict, an ecclesiastical censure that would prohibit the celebration of mass, the administration of the sacraments and Christian burial, if Banzer did not call an end to the attacks and accept the demands of the strikers.

The next day, a girl appeared at Iriarte's house to ask for his help because her father had been arrested.

'In fact, she was an agent who had been sent to check if I was at home. Half a block away was a jeep belonging to the Ministry of the Interior. She went to tell the police I was in, so they could arrest me. I realized what was going on and decided to get out because Marcelo Quiroga Santa Cruz, the founder of the Socialist Party, was hiding in my house and I didn't want them to find him. So I came out and they arrested me.'

He was taken to an office in the Ministry of the Interior. The captain opened a tall cupboard, removed all the files and other papers it contained, and pushed Iriarte inside. There was just enough space to stand upright. He couldn't sit down or even squat.

'It was terrible. I thought I was suffocating, I had a panic attack. Even today, I can smell the dust inside that cupboard. They put me inside it at half past one in the afternoon and kept me there until nine o'clock in the evening.'

One of the policemen standing guard over Iriarte was afraid the priest was going to asphyxiate and, taking care not to be seen by the captain, he wedged the door open with a piece of cardboard. At nine, when the officers left, the three policemen who were watching over Iriarte opened the cupboard and offered him the captain's chair.

'We're sorry, Father. The captain is a very bad man.'

Iriarte remembers that they had a friendly chat.

'In Bolivia, that's what happens. Despite everything there's always an element of humanity. I said, "They must pay you a lot to do such a horrible job." "No," they answered, "but there's nothing else. It's the only work we can get." "Well, I'll find you a job when I get out of here."

All three of them gave me their names and their phone numbers. "Please, Father, help us find a job ..." One of them went off to get me a blanket. He came back with a colleague, who also gave me his number in the hope that I could find him a job, too.'

At three in the morning, Iriarte was woken up and taken to see the minister of the interior, Brigadier General Gallo. The minister greeted the priest, apologized for his ordeal, invited him to take a seat and told him in a quiet voice:

'Father, General Banzer has just resigned.'

Then he informed Iriarte that he was free to go.

'I went out and the streets were full of people who had been released from the cells. We had a huge party, we hugged each other and we cried. The miners' wives had won a great victory.'

* * *

'Democracy owes the miners' wives a lot. We were always there in the struggle, in the strikes, we never gave up. But to society, we're invisible. We're invisible to the miners. Our own husbands ignore us.'

Dora Camacho is forty-eight years old. She's small, and wears her jet-black hair tied back in a ponytail. We're drinking tea in a café in the centre of Oruro. She was born in a mining camp in Cataricagua, the daughter of a miner who fell ill and died when she was only ten. She married young and her husband was laid off when Comibol was dismantled in 1986. He emigrated to Peru to find work, but now he is employed by Inti Raymi, a private mining company that exploits the mineral deposits near Oruro. According to Camacho, the private company has better technology and is more attentive to the safety of its workers, in contrast with the disastrous situation in the cooperatives. Camacho is the president of the National Committee of Miners' Housewives: the organization that was founded after the successful hunger strike of 1961, the organization that was led by Domitila Barrios, the organization that overthrew Banzer. She sips her tea. Her voice is calm but resolute, her gaze both tired and wise.

> In our association, we aren't miners but we run the households of mining families. There's so much poverty, so much loneliness, lots of women are widowed or have to bring up their children alone because their husbands have abandoned them. They have nothing, they have to sell snacks in the street or find work as cleaners and leave their children on their own. If they get sick, what do they do for money? We fight for our rights because we are also workers, and we fight for the rights of our husbands. But even so, there are men who don't respect us. There's a lot of sexism. And violence is a huge problem. The violence in the mines is terrible.

The Miners' Federation invites the housewives to its national conferences; its representatives can speak, but they have no vote. Camacho says that something is better than nothing, that in some mines they don't even allow the housewives' committee to operate.

A few streets away there is an allegorical statue of a woman who strides forward, her arm raised high, her gaze fixed on the horizon. The plaque reads, 'The National Federation of Feminine Christian Associations of Bolivia, in homage to the most beautiful of the Supreme Creator's works: Woman'. It is dated 11 October 1977, a few weeks before the four miners' wives ...

(four beautiful works of the Supreme Creator)

... started the hunger strike that toppled Banzer.

On the outskirts of Oruro is the highest religious sculpture on the planet, an image of *la Virgen del Socavón*, Our Lady of the Mineshaft. Situated at 3,845 metres above sea level, she stands 45 metres tall and was inaugurated on 1 February 2013 with the blessing of Pope Benedict XVI and a speech delivered by President Evo Morales. Our Lady of the Mineshaft cost 1.3 million dollars to build and incorporates 1,500 tons of metal, concrete and ferro-cement. Inside are eight floors with windows so that visitors can look out on the city below. In her arms she cradles a two-ton Baby Jesus. She is the maternal image to which the miners pray for protection and help.

'We send reports to the ministry,' says Camacho,

we demand an audience. We tell them they have to monitor the cooperatives because they exploit the miners. They hire peasants for short periods, a few weeks, a few months, and they don't provide safety equipment. The peasants go down the mine in sandals! They're paid next to nothing, have no contract, no insurance, and the work is very dangerous. It's exploitation, pure and simple. And the cooperatives send kids down the mine. So everyone's wages are lower. We call on the ministry to monitor the situation, we write reports, we document violations, we do a lot of work. All of it for free, unselfishly.

At the last assembly of the Miners' Federation, Camacho asked every miner to contribute one peso a year to support the housewives' committee.

'It's the least the men could give us. We're fighting for their rights. But we still have to struggle, even for one miserable peso.'

* * *

Gregorio Iriarte received another phone call on 22 March 1980. His friend, Luis Espinal – Jesuit, journalist and cinema critic – had disappeared. Espinal had worked with Iriarte to establish the Assembly of Human Rights, had helped organize the hunger strike that overthrew Banzer, and had penned articles that were fiercely critical of successive dictatorships.

Espinal had gone to the cinema and had not returned.

Iriarte went to his house. In Espinal's bedroom, Iriarte found an open notebook containing the last text Espinal had written. The title: 'No more martyrs'.

Our country needs builders, not martyrs. The martyr is showy, over-emotional, he thinks too much of himself. The martyr is the last adventurer, an individualist, a masochist. If he cannot glory in his triumph, he strives to shine in defeat. He enjoys being misunderstood and persecuted. He needs the torturer, unconsciously creating him. Is the martyr a weakling? He lacks the stamina to live as a revolutionary and that's why he wants to die, in the hope of becoming an exhibit in a display cabinet. Because the martyr has something of the poser, something of the bullfighter. The people, by contrast, do not wish to be martyrs. When the people fall in combat they do so silently, they fall without posing, they do not dream of being commemorated by statues. We need politicians, engineers, workers of the revolution, not martyrs. We should give our lives working, not dying. Down with the slogans that glorify death. Someone once said: heavy burdens are carried by oxen, not eagles.

They found his corpse the next day, abandoned on the outskirts of La Paz. He had been tortured in the municipal slaughterhouse, his chest burned with a branding iron before they despatched him with twelve bullets.

The work, once more, of Klaus Barbie's paramilitaries. They assassinated Espinal. They assassinated the socialist leader, Quiroga Santa Cruz, the one who had sought refuge in Iriarte's house and was exposing the crimes and corruption of General Banzer in parliament. They assassinated Father Mauricio Lefebvre, a defender of human rights. They bombed journalists, lawyers and left-wing politicians. And in July 1980 they orchestrated a coup that brought the army back to power. The new president was General García Meza, and the minister of the interior was Colonel Arce Gómez, another graduate of the School of the Americas, who appeared on television to issue the following message to his opponents:

'When you go out, make sure you have a copy of your will in your pocket.'

Iriarte hid in a convent and wrote a book which was published anonymously: *Narcotráfico y política*, narco-trafficking and politics. It described in great detail how President García Meza and his minister of the interior directed a huge business exporting Bolivian coca to Colombia, an enterprise which encompassed the fields where the crop was grown, processing plants in the jungle and a fleet of light aircraft. The business had an annual turnover of three billion dollars – an eighth of the country's GDP – and Bolivia was a narco-state at the service of the army. Iriarte also published a famous 'List of Bolivian paramilitaries and foreign mercenaries', with hundreds of names, information, connections and photos: hundreds of members of the Internacional Negra, a far-right terrorist alliance active in Europe and America at the time, whom Barbie had welcomed to Bolivia to support the military dictatorship and its cocaine business.

The assassinations, the looting, the drug-trafficking and the Nazi displays got so out of hand that high-ranking army officers eventually tried to bring the situation under control. There were accusations of corruption, uprisings, changes of power, military juntas that sought to provide a veneer of respectability but were unable to govern a country that was falling apart in their hands. They called a general election in 1982.

With democracy finally restored, the Bolivian government extradited Barbie to France, where he was sentenced to life imprisonment for crimes against humanity. He died in prison in 1991. García Meza and Arce Gómez were put on trial and were both sentenced to thirty years in prison for their numerous crimes. They are still in jail.

Iriarte, meanwhile, spent thirty more years campaigning and writing. He died in Cochabamba in 2012. The cause of his death was one he would never have predicted: old age.

4

The Dumping
Ground

At dawn, groups of women sweep back and forth across
the slopes like flocks of dark birds. They are breaking
rocks, pecking away at the mountain with their mallets,
the sound echoing over the Cerro Rico. The scene is
repeated day after day, as if they are determined to chip
away the whole mountain until nothing but a few grains
of stone are left.

Alicia takes a bag with some sandwiches and a flask of
tea to the *canchamina*, 4,500 metres up, where her aunt
Lorena sits breaking rocks with two other women. Lorena
introduces me to Rosario and Luisa, both members of the
guards' association. We shake hands, my own skin feeling
soft against their calloused palms.

'We went to the provincial government, to protest.'

'Were you carrying dynamite?'

'No! Maybe next time!'

As president of the association of guards and *palliris*
for the La Plata sector, Lorena met the public prosecutor

and provincial government officials in Potosí. She described their terrible working conditions and explained how the women don't even earn the minimum monthly wage of 815 pesos (approximately 135 dollars). The co-ops pay them 400 to 500 pesos for their work as guards, allow the women to pick over the discarded rock, and provide the adobe huts where they live.

'But it's not enough, it's not enough to feed and clothe a family. I have seven children.'

Lorena points towards the slope.

'You've seen where we live. It's very polluted. At night, when the Manquiri plant is operating, black smoke blows into our homes and stings our eyes. Our kids are always sick; they have headaches, stomach aches, diarrhoea.'

The Manquiri plant processes the slag that has accumulated on the slopes of Cerro Rico after decades of mining, performing the same job as the women, but with industrial machinery instead of hammers. The silver it extracts is made into ingots, generating income of around 200 million dollars per year, according to the Ministry of Mining.

Manquiri is a subsidiary of Coeur Mining, a US multinational which exploits a classic loophole: the Bolivian state grants the mining cooperatives a licence to work the deposits, charging very little tax because of the 'social nature' of these enterprises, and some cooperatives then transfer these licences to the multinationals. Seven Potosí co-ops leased their holdings on Cerro Rico to Manquiri. Across the country, thirty-one cooperatives repeated this ploy with other companies. In September 2016, the government annulled the contracts on the basis that 'private companies and an elite group of cooperative managers' were enriching themselves by exploiting the advantageous terms offered to the co-ops but without respecting the underlying principles. The cooperatives are, in theory, associations of workers who share risks, benefits and profits, and have the right to participate in decisions. The cooperatives are meant to have a commitment to the communities in which they operate. They are not meant to be a front for multinationals. Although respect for the environment is one of the principles the cooperatives are meant to observe, four out of five cooperatives regularly breach basic environmental legislation, according to research by Emilio Madrid.

'I see my grandchildren playing in the earth,' says Lorena. 'Their skin is stained, their hands are covered with warts, their snot turns black.

'We protest but the co-ops just ignore us. They look down on us, and mock us for trying to organize. And they get angry if they find out we've been down to the Care Centre to learn to make ponchos, bags and blankets to sell at the market for some extra cash.

'If they find out, they tell us off. The cooperatives want us here all the time, working for peanuts.'

Many of the mining co-ops aren't cooperatives at all; they're just vehicles for fraud and exploitation. Anything from 25 to 80 per cent of their workers are not members and have no right to participate in decisions or to share in the profits of the enterprise. They are seasonal workers, guards, *palliris*, children, casual workers who earn an average of 260 dollars a month and, according to the United Nations Development Programme, 'aren't provided with safety equipment and don't have health insurance or pensions. The wages they receive are lower than in other industries.'

At the same time, a caste of senior managers has emerged who are, in reality, nothing more than private businessmen in disguise: they don't work in the mines, they exploit their labourers, and they rake off a huge share of the profits – as much as 100,000 pesos a month (around 17,000 dollars) according to Kirsten Francescone and Vladimir Díaz of the Bolivia Documentation and Information Centre (CEDIB). These managers exploit the benefits available to the cooperatives – the state grants them licences, provides them with materials and equipment, subsidizes them, writes off their debts and gives them preferential tax treatment – and then they act like private businessmen, signing contracts with foreign firms to lease out their licences. These are the bosses who drive around in Hummers, build luxury houses in exclusive districts, and appear on lists of Bolivian millionaires. They are extremely powerful, because they control the federations of cooperatives, representing tens of thousands of workers (tens of thousands of voters), they hold senior positions in the country's political parties, and they occupy posts in both regional and central government. At their peak, they controlled the Ministry of Mining. If the government proposes a law they don't like – a law forcing them to allow their workers to join trade unions, for example – they are powerful enough to stop it. They block roads, paralyse cities and generally get what they want.

In 1985, the Bolivian government privatized and liberalized the economy in one fell swoop. As a result, the number of mining cooperatives proliferated, creating a convenient dumping ground for thousands of surplus workers.

* * *

On 29 August 1985, the new president appeared on television to address the Bolivian people. Something remarkable had just happened: for the first time in the country's 160-year history, one democratically elected government had peacefully handed over power to another democratically elected government of a different political stripe. When the military dictatorship relinquished its grip on power in 1982, Siles Zuazo won the free elections that followed, and ruled as president for three years. When he lost the presidential election of 1985, he ceded power to his rival. The new head of state was none other than Paz Estenssoro, the same man who had led the 1952 revolution. He had an uncompromising message:

'Fellow citizens, our homeland is dying. Unless we show the moral courage to engage in a new form of politics and to endure the sacrifices this will entail, Bolivia will die.'

He went on to announce his emergency remedy: Supreme Decree 21.060, a monumental piece of legislation that would transform the country at a stroke. It comprised 220 laws to privatize state-owned enterprises and liberalize the economy. Neither the voters nor the members of parliament nor even Paz Estenssoro's own ministers (with the exception of his two closest confidants) had any idea that the decree was being drawn up. The legislation – which went against the manifesto on which the president had been elected – had been compiled by a committee of economists under the supervision of advisers from Washington, in a series of secret meetings at a mansion belonging to Senator Gonzalo Sánchez de Lozada. In addition to his political position, the senator was the owner of Bolivia's largest private mining company and was the richest man in the country; he was also the new minister of the economy.

In 1993, Sánchez de Lozada was elected president, and oversaw another wave of privatizations, as the country's oil, gas, mining and electricity companies were sold off to the private sector at bargain-basement prices, the whole process shrouded in a fog of fraud and evasion, the wheels greased by corruption and bribery. The president snapped up a state-owned smelting firm for a mere six million dollars. Three years later, he sold it to a US multinational – for ninety million. When demonstrations broke out in 2003, Sánchez de Lozada sent the army in to put down the protests by force. By the time they had finished, there were 67 dead and 400 wounded. Several ministers resigned, a crowd stormed the presidential palace, and the president fled in a helicopter. He went into exile in the United States, a fugitive from Bolivian justice, accused of responsibility for torture and extrajudicial killings.

Another participant in those urgent secret meetings at Sánchez de Lozada's mansion was the former dictator, Hugo Banzer. He had also run for the presidency in 1985 and had topped the popular vote. However, Banzer failed to win an absolute majority, and Paz Estenssoro's alliance with left-wing parties in the congress gave him the presidency. Despite this setback, Banzer continued to wield a lot of influence and it was his American economic adviser, Jeffrey Sachs, who designed Supreme Decree 21.060. Paz Estenssoro accepted the proposals of his political rival because it was the only way for the bankrupt country to access loans from the International Monetary Fund.

Bolivia's infant democracy was under pressure to pay back the huge debts that had been racked up by the military dictators. Over the preceding decades, the United States and the big banks had offered generous loans to the military strongmen, seeing them as partners in the struggle against communism and sponsors of laws that were advantageous to the oil and gas multinationals. The dictators used these loans to build highways, factories and hospitals in order to convince the people that the regime was on their side. Highways, factories and hospitals whose costs spiralled out of control, the construction work often unfinished, with nobody to check on standards or spending, or to notice that millions of dollars were being diverted into the pockets of presidents, ministers, businessmen and army officers. During the seven years of the Banzer dictatorship, Bolivia's foreign debt rose from 460 to 3,000 million dollars. But its creditors didn't bat an eyelid.

At the start of the 1980s, the US Federal Reserve began to raise its interest rates – from 8 per cent to more than 20 per cent – causing the borrowing costs of Latin American countries to balloon. At the same time, these countries' income fell as a result of the collapse in the price of commodities. Such as tin. The United States repeated a classic move from its playbook, offloading 30,000 tons of reserves and causing the market to crash. Bolivia was deprived of its main source of hard currency. At which point, the United States demanded that the country repay its debts. And the democratic government obliged.

As a result, when Paz Estenssoro came to power in 1985, the country was bankrupt. The amount required to service the interest on its external debt – not the debt itself, just the annual interest – was more than the entire Bolivian national budget. On the eve of the 1985 elections, the US ambassador, Edwin Corr, had warned all the candidates that new loans would only be provided in exchange for the complete liberalization of the economy.

Responsibility for the plan was assigned to Sachs, an up-and-coming academic who specialized in hyperinflation. In Bolivia, the annual inflation rate for 1985 was 8,170 per cent. The only thing the Bolivian peso was good for was wallpaper. If you were going out for a couple of beers, it was wise to order them both at the same time, otherwise the price would have gone up by the time you'd finished the first one. To bring inflation under control and increase earnings, Sachs put forward some radical measures. The state stopped printing money to cover the gaps in its finances. It put up taxes on petrol and basic goods, removed food subsidies, cut back its spending on pensions, health and education, laid off thousands of public employees, and froze the salaries of the rest. And it stopped regulating prices, exchange rates or collective bargaining agreements.

Several of Paz Estenssoro's ministers, worried by the extreme nature of these measures, wanted to resign. Bedregal – one of the two ministers who had been privy to the plan – confronted them and argued, 'We have to be like the pilot who dropped the bomb on Hiroshima. When he released the atomic bomb, he didn't know what he was doing, but as soon as he saw the mushroom cloud, he said, "Oh my God! I'm so sorry!" And that's exactly what we have to do: implement these measures first and apologize afterwards.' The Bolivian trade union confederation called a two-week strike and the government responded with a state of emergency that lasted three months. It banned political gatherings, arrested 1,500 demonstrators and, in keeping with tradition, exiled 200 trade union leaders to the Amazon. 'This time, they didn't take us to the jungle to torture and murder us,' wrote workers' leader Filemón

Escóbar, 'but they kept us captive for long enough to ensure they could implement their economic plan without any opposition.'

In the name of an untrammelled free market, the decree also abolished state subsidies for local producers and eliminated import duties, ignoring the fact that the imported goods often came from rich countries that continued to subsidize their own producers.

With these measures, Bolivia brought inflation under control, balanced its budget, was praised by the IMF and was heralded as an exemplar of market economics. It continued to sell its raw materials in their basic state, using cheap labour, without developing local industry, and buying almost everything Bolivians needed from other countries. As a reward, the country was allowed to renegotiate its debt and was given more time to meet its payments. The economy began to grow and the result was referred to as the Bolivian economic miracle.

The country was, once again, a guinea pig. The IMF injected it with an experimental liberalization programme – which would subsequently be applied elsewhere – and sat back to observe the results. In his memoirs, Sachs recounts that he arrived in Bolivia without even knowing where it was on the map, with 'an empty notebook' and 'a basic theoretical understanding' of problems that nobody had taught him to address. There he discovered, on the job, that 'hyperinflation, and the budget deficit that had caused it, were symptoms of much deeper ills' and that 'the end of hyperinflation did not mean the end of suffering or extreme poverty'. 'Fortunately,' he added, 'in my first foray into country advising, this serious mistake did not cause too much disruption.'

Perhaps he wasn't asking the right people.

The economy grew, but not fast enough to end the country's economic hardship. A few Bolivians became richer; the majority became substantially poorer. Thousands lost their jobs, many others continued to work but in terrible conditions: for low wages, with no job security, and with huge cuts to their pensions and their unemployment and health benefits. Poverty became even more widespread.

The logical free market response was to shift into the sole viable sector of the economy: thousands of Bolivians took to cocaine production, the only activity that was truly profitable. In a few years, the percentage of peasants cultivating coca leaf rose from 17 to 37 per cent, the area of land given over to coca bushes expanded dramatically, and illegal exports of the drug generated more income than all the country's legal exports put together. One person in every ten worked in coca cultivation or cocaine production. According to the political scientists Catherine Conaghan and James Malloy, 'the drug trade (like the international aid that Estenssoro received) helped soften the blows of stabilization. In addition to generating income, the injection of "coca-dollars" ... helped stabilize the currency.'

The idea was that market liberalization and the creation of private companies would absorb the thousands of workers laid off by the public sector. But the only people offering employment were the cocaine producers. Bolivia remained locked in its traditional role as a country without infrastructure, investment or industry: a country that was little more than a transient camp for the extraction of oil, gas and minerals. Just as in the previous 500 years. A country that was unable to defend itself against the international speculators who gamble with the prices of raw materials and ruin entire countries, knowing little, caring less.

On 24 October 1985 it was Bolivia's turn. The price of tin crashed and the London Metal Exchange suspended trading. It cost Comibol ten dollars to produce one pound of tin, a pound of tin which sold for only two dollars. The state-owned enterprise had already been pushed to the verge of bankruptcy by incompetent management, corruption, obsolete equipment and the declining profitability of deposits that were all but worked out. The collapse in the price of tin tipped the company over the edge. The government took drastic measures: it abandoned all the mines bar one, and laid off 22,793 miners out of a total workforce of 27,522.

Because there was no other way to make a living in Bolivia, the miners continued to support themselves in the only way they could, shifting en masse into the private mining sector. The government announced legal incentives for the cooperatives – which they presented as a commitment to private enterprise – allowing unemployed miners to organize themselves into small groups of entrepreneurs who would resume production. The state granted them licences to work the ore deposits; it gave them loans, offered tax concessions, and turned a blind eye to violations of environmental and employment legislation. Hundreds of cooperatives sprang up: teams of miners who lacked plans or technology, exploiting deposits that were no longer profitable for big industry but which could still be worked by those willing to extract the ore, stone by stone.

They earned a pittance and often paid for the privilege with their lives.

And, to help make ends meet, their children left school and went down the mine.

There was nothing out of the ordinary about the collapse in the price of tin; it was just the spirit of the times. Between 1984 and 1987 the speculators who gambled on the prices of commodities such as rice, wheat, sugar, cocoa, coffee, timber, cotton and metals produced 140 price shocks (sudden falls of more than 10 per cent), according to Naomi Klein. In the global market, there are no rules restricting sales or purchases. Banks, investment funds and speculators move huge sums of money from one corner of the globe to another, from one stock exchange to another, from one currency to another, from one commodity to another, with the aim of making money on their transactions, causing some prices to rise and others to fall. They can cause the price of wheat to rise, earn huge profits – and condemn millions to hunger. They can cause the price of tin to fall, ruin a country that depends on it for income – and then force the same country to sign agreements to save itself from catastrophe.

'Everything we did from 1983 onwards was based on our new sense of mission to have the south privatized or die; towards this end we ignominiously created economic bedlam in Latin America ... in 1983 to 1988.' These are the words of Davison Budhoo, IMF economist and one of the people responsible for designing economic liberalization plans for a plethora of African and Latin American countries during the 1980s. Poor countries were buffeted by the speculators. And just when they could take no more, the IMF, the World Bank and the US Treasury Department stepped in, offering loans in exchange for implementing a programme of privatization, deregulation and cuts in social spending, reducing the state to a minimum and removing its capacity to redistribute wealth and protect the vulnerable, eliminating any restrictions on the entry of foreign goods and foreign companies. Years later, some IMF and World Bank economists argued that the wave of privatization and liberalization had nothing to do with economic stabilization. Instead, they were simply taking advantage of the economic crisis which they themselves had engineered to impose these 'solutions', to open up these countries to multinationals and an unregulated global market in which speculators could make huge profits.

* * *

Governments and traders speculate in commodities. Their game ruins underdeveloped countries, and these countries then accept international aid and the conditions which come attached. For example, they refrain from regulating relations between companies and their workers, refrain from monitoring industrial activity and, at the end of it all, a twelve-year-old girl goes down the mine.

* * *

'When it closed down, Comibol removed all its equipment from the mines,' wrote Jocelyn Michard in his study of the cooperative mining sector. 'At the time, the work was highly mechanized: there were electric drills and the ore was removed in motorized trucks running along underground railway lines. The galleries were wide and had electric lighting, and the mines had offices and health stations. None of it was left behind: Comibol even ripped up the rails.' The state-owned company wanted to sell its technology to the cooperative members, but the equipment was old and the asking prices so high that few miners were willing or able to pay them. 'Vast quantities of equipment – drills, grinders, even entire processing plants – were abandoned, left to rust,' Michard explains, 'while the miners worked by hand.'

'The equipment was replaced by miners' lungs,' wrote the engineer and former mining minister Jorge Espinoza.

Prior to 1985, there had been 20,000 cooperative members: one quarter of the total Bolivian mining workforce. By 2016, they numbered 119,000, almost 90 per cent of the total, compared to the 8,000 who worked in the private mining sector and the 7,500 who were still employed by the state. This was what 'liberalization' meant for most workers: losing stable jobs and being transferred to the informal sector, where they lacked contracts and security, and the work was performed under dreadful conditions.

In 2012, only one third of the 1,300 mining cooperatives were 'semi-mechanized', according to Isaac Meneses, deputy minister for mining cooperatives. Semi-mechanized just means they use electric drills at the rock face; the rest of the work can be done by hand. The other two-thirds of the cooperative sector don't even use drills for this: they dislodge the rock with hammers and chisels, load it into sacks or wagons, break it up with mallets, crush it with rollers, and separate out the ore using acid baths, which they stir by hand. Humans working with the brute force of animals.

Such methods are extremely inefficient. According to a study by the Pazos Kanki Foundation, each of Sumimoto Corporation's employees produces the same as ninety-four miners working for cooperatives using artisanal methods. And because their productivity is so low, the cooperative members use other workers who are in an even weaker position: casual labourers, widows who split rocks with mallets, children.

Cerro Rico de Potosí has some of the worst statistics: 80 per cent of its miners are employed on a casual basis. Of these, some 700 are children and adolescents, 5 per cent of the labour force according to research by Laura Baas, although figures are hard to come by and vary widely.

The cooperatives look the other way.

And the state pulled out of the mines. They no longer have anything to do with such problems.

* * *

Polonio Chiri walks across a patch of stony ground halfway up a mountain in Catavi, not far from Potosí. Polonio is a security guard, responsible for protecting a ruin. He wears a blue helmet and a khaki jacket with orange reflective bands, and makes his way very slowly around the skeleton of a dismantled factory. He wanders among crumbling walls, exposed beams, doors hanging on their hinges, conveyor belts that end in mid-air. When the wind blows, the factory creaks and groans as if it is finally about to collapse. It makes you afraid to sneeze. Or to cough. And Polonio coughs a lot.

He is a wiry forty-five-year-old, with a nervous smile. And he has silicosis. But he doesn't like taking his pills.

'They leave me feeling all drugged up,' he says, before clearing his throat noisily.

On the right-hand pocket of his jacket is an embroidered crest: *Catavi Mining Company. Comibol. Bolivia.* On the left-hand pocket, a small national flag: red, yellow and green. He takes his pills when there's no alternative, when he has one of those coughing fits that goes on all night, when he thinks he might have cracked one of his ribs from so much coughing. Sometimes he feels as if his skeleton is crumbling like the factory. And he takes his pills. He holds on, breathes a little more easily, manages to snatch some sleep, and in the morning he gets dressed, puts on his boots, has breakfast and goes off, exhausted, to work – as a security guard at a ruined factory.

The hours go by. He sits on a plastic chair, outside a metal hut, and every now and then he wanders across the stony ground, under the sun, and does a circuit of the 'sink and float' plant.

'Sink and float' was the technique they used to separate the ore from the slag, the lighter impurities floating on top, the denser tin sinking to the bottom. Three shifts of workers kept the plant operating around the clock, receiving the trucks from the mines, concentrating the mineral, and sending it on by train. When Comibol abandoned the factory in 1986, hordes of former miners ransacked it for everything they could find.

'They took the beams, the corrugated iron, even the nuts and bolts.'

I'm not quite sure what this man is guarding. Nothing but junk is left. Surely it would be better if the miners were allowed to finish digesting this factory and move on? Perhaps the only thing that remains is the dignity of the last employee, Polonio Chiri.

'I make sure the co-op miners don't steal anything else. When they have to prop up the galleries, they don't buy timber because it's expensive. They come here and cut through the girders, and carry them off.'

The factory is like a ship adrift on a sea of slag. On their knees, three miners are picking over it for rocks.

'They belong to the 23 March Cooperative,' explains Polonio. 'They take the leftovers, the stuff nobody wanted before. It's the same inside the mine. Now, they just find the odd thread of ore. I've seen huge seams in my day' – he spreads his arms wide – 'with 57 per cent purity, incredible, but back then tin was only fetching one dollar eighty to the pound, it was a disaster. Between 1993 and 1994, we spent over a year drilling into the hill, at a loss. We went 150 metres before we hit the seam. But the price was too low. Then the seam broke off and we couldn't pick it up again.'

Polonio retired with silicosis and Comibol offered him this job as a watchman.

'It's temporary. So far, they've always renewed my contract. I wish they'd give me a permanent job but I can't complain, because with the illness I can't work inside the mine and at least here I can make some money.'

I ask him how much he earns.

'Not much.'

Near the ruined factory, 100 metres away, there's a military barracks.

'The army used to look after the factory, but then the soldiers tore it to pieces. They took everything and sold it. This factory should be operating and creating work, but between one side and the other they've taken everything.'

The army painted murals on the barrack walls. One of them reads, 'Bolivian Army. The forge of the nation.' Next to it is painted a savage face, a furious gorilla baring its fangs and wearing a helmet marked with the letters PM, *policía militar*. Near by is another slogan: 'I only believe in God and the Bolivian Army. So long as I believe in them, I fear neither my enemies nor death.' And an enigmatic piece of graffiti: 'If a child kills, he does so out of bravery. Don't be tempted to imitate him. Killing is only for the brave.'

'Sometimes people who used to work in the factory come up here,' Polonio says. 'They come out of curiosity. And they cry. I've seen lots of them in tears.'

* * *

The old problem: what is to be done with the surplus workers? And what is to be done if we'd like to have them at hand, just in case we need them again in the future? It would be convenient if they were engaged in a similar activity, something they could do for themselves, earning just enough to survive. Without doing too well, without having other jobs, other trades, other ways of earning a living.

After the Great Crash of 1929, ore prices plummeted (just as they would do again in 1985) and Bolivian companies laid off thousands of miners (just like in 1985) and the unemployed miners were organized into cooperatives that continued to scrape away at deposits that were no longer profitable for the big companies to exploit (just like in 1985). The first miners' cooperative was created in Potosí in 1939 to work the marginal zones that had been abandoned by the companies. Lacking technology and investment, the co-op members constituted a reserve labour force, able to survive but not to prosper while they waited for a second chance: if the prices went back up, perhaps the companies that had dismissed them would hire them again. They had no alternative. At the time, the Bolivian mining sector was generating vast wealth but the profits were never used to diversify the economy or to smooth the path to development. The government was in the hands of the mining oligarchs, and the only investments it made were those that suited the three large mining companies and kept ninety-eight of every hundred Bolivians in poverty. A cheap, disposable labour force on whose backs one could sow turnips.

After the tin crisis of 1985, the solution was the same: thousands of workers lost their jobs and turned to the cooperative sector.

According to economist Pablo Poveda, cooperative members account for 90 per cent of the Bolivian mining workforce ... and generate 3.29 per cent of the industry's output.

At the same time, the San Cristóbal open-cast mine in Potosí extracts vast quantities of silver, lead and zinc. Between 2009 and 2012, it produced half of Bolivia's total mining output. It is operated by a Japanese multinational, Sumimoto, which uses the very latest technology. 'Private companies tear up and process whole mountains without wasting time sifting through the rock,' writes Michard.

San Cristóbal employs a thousand workers. At the same time, there are 120,000 miners who are deemed expendable: the mass of co-op members, day labourers and *palliris* who destroy their health as they hack away at the rocks, earning just enough to keep starvation at bay and whose contribution to the sector is a mere 3 per cent. They could disappear and the system wouldn't even notice.

In fact, many of them do disappear. And nobody even notices.

* * *

Alicia's father, Nicolás, died of silicosis at the age of thirty-four. The air in the galleries is thick with silica particles, the miners inhale them constantly, the particles adhere to their lungs and form nodules, small fibrous balls that block the miners' bronchial tubes and obstruct their breathing. After ten or fifteen years of inhaling silica, almost all the miners are suffocated by the disease. There are scarcely any healthy miners aged thirty-five.

When Nicolás had to give up work because he couldn't breathe, he was cut off without a peso. He was a peasant who had migrated to the mines and been taken on as a casual labourer, but he never became a cooperative member.

'He didn't have any papers,' Rosa explains.

When her husband couldn't work any more, the situation became desperate. With her two oldest children, she started breaking stones to earn some money. Alicia was still too young to work. She was eight when her father died.

'I never got a widow's pension,' says Rosa. 'We had nothing, no pension, no insurance, nothing. I was left alone with four kids. The co-op gave me this job and let us live up here on the *canchamina*.'

* * *

Ibeth Garabito goes from funeral to funeral in Potosí enquiring about the dead. There is no register of miners' deaths from accident or disease, no reports, no numbers. The reason is simple. If nobody knows how many people have disappeared or why they've disappeared, nobody has to take responsibility.

The local newspapers frequently publish reports of accidents in the mine. An eighteen-year-old crushed by a rockfall; a twenty-two-year-old who fell 80 metres down a shaft, leaving his ruined body unrecognizable, according to his brother, who was working with him at the time and explains that the victim had no insurance; two workers aged twenty-four and thirty-one who died when twelve sticks of dynamite they had just finished placing went off prematurely, leaving two orphaned children.

Occasionally, there are a few statistics. UNESCO counted 120 deaths on Cerro Rico in 2010. The departmental director of employment states that six of every ten accidents in the mine are not recorded and that the colleagues of victims are often bribed or threatened into silence. Only 10 per cent of mining companies have workplace safety guidelines, according to mining engineer Alfredo Gutiérrez. The number of accidents in the cooperative sector is far higher than in the private or state sectors, according to another engineer, Carlos Sandy.

Ibeth Garabito continues. 'In the cemetery records, I realized that many of those who die in the mines are registered as farm workers, because they are migrants from the countryside, and that way they aren't recorded as mining deaths. And the ones that die of silicosis aren't included either, because they don't die in the mines so they don't count.'

Garabito is chair of an organization called Musol (Women's Solidarity) and she explains another reason why the deaths are hidden: to deny widows and orphans their rights.

We investigate and do our own calculations: in Potosí, an average of fourteen miners die every month from illness or accident. That leaves fourteen widows, with an average of five children in their care, and they receive nothing. The majority of the victims are not covered by the law, they don't have contracts, so their wives aren't entitled to receive a widow's pension. And even when they are entitled, they often don't know about it or they are cheated or threatened. The cooperative lawyers propose lopsided agreements, persuading the widows to renounce their rights or to accept a quarter of what they are owed by law. We recently filed a complaint against a lawyer who convinced a widow he had done her a favour by obtaining five hundred dollars' worth of compensation, of which he withheld three hundred dollars for services rendered. This kind of fraud perpetuates the cycle of exploitation, because the orphans are left with no choice but to work in the mine from an early age, under appalling conditions.

* * *

Rosario Tapia directs the League for the Defence of the Environment, the organization that analysed blood samples from Cerro Rico residents and found very high concentrations of arsenic, cadmium, mercury, zinc and chrome.

You look into the causes of miners' deaths and on the certificate it says, 'due to cardiorespiratory failure'. Well, in the end everyone dies of cardiorespiratory failure. Miners fall down shafts, are crushed by rock, are poisoned by gas; above all, they die from silicosis. Everyone's heart gives way in the end but nobody gives any details because that would make it possible to identify responsibilities. And that's before we talk about the families who live on the Cerro, in terrible conditions – hunger, cold, pollution. Lots of people die of TB, for example. They're very weak and all sorts of diseases can finish them off. But that's not recorded anywhere. The cooperatives and the state just cover it up. They don't want us to know the true cost of mining.

* * *

The streets near the public hospital in Potosí are overflowing with four-wheel-drive vehicles: huge futuristic tanks in silver or metallic blue, tyres as high as a man's waist, with smoked-glass windows and shiny chrome accessories. The favoured choice of mining bosses. They park as close to the hospital as possible. The roads – and the pavements – are clogged with Toyota Highlanders, Chevrolet Silverados, Nissan Terranos.

In the waiting room of the Respiratory Diseases Department, men in baseball caps sit coughing. One of them has an oxygen tank on a trolley by his side.

I tell the woman on the reception desk that I'm a journalist and I'd like to talk to a lung specialist about miners' health, about silicosis. She calls Dr Gualberto Astorga and tells me to go through. The doctor is waiting for me at the door of his office, and asks me to come back the day after tomorrow, Thursday afternoon, because he has an outpatient clinic today.

I return on Thursday afternoon but he tells me it's not a good time because he has patients to see. I ask him if I could steal a few minutes of his time at the end of the day, but he says he can't talk to journalists outside the hospital. He tells me to come back the next day, Friday afternoon.

I turn up on Friday afternoon, and this time I think I'm in luck: the waiting room is empty. I knock on the door, Dr Astorga tells me to come in, but his face falls when he sees it's me. He says he can't talk to the press without permission from his superiors. I need to ask for written permission from the hospital management. They're based in another building, but not far away.

I go outside, find the other building, enter and explain my problem to a receptionist. The receptionist sends me up to a secretary's office on the second floor. I explain what I need. The secretary calls Dr Martínez and shows me through. I explain my situation to Dr Martínez: I'm a journalist, I want to ask Dr Astorga some questions about miners' health, Dr Astorga says he's willing to answer my questions but needs permission in writing from the management.

Dr Martínez laughs.

'Written authorization?'

He gets up and asks me to follow him. We walk down a corridor and he gives me an encouraging slap on the back. We go into another office, he puts a sheet of paper into a Torpedo typewriter, types up the following note, signs it and stamps it in blue ink.

FAO: Dr Gualberto Astorga
Pulmonologist

Please provide every assistance to the bearer of this letter, who is studying the life and customs of our patients who work in the mining industry.

Yours sincerely,

Dr José Luis Martínez Márquez

Regional Medical Director

Public Health System

Dr Martínez hands me the piece of paper, smiles again and wishes me luck. I leave the building, return to the Respiratory Diseases Department and take a seat in the waiting room. After a quarter of an hour, the door opens and a patient comes out. I approach and say hello to Dr Astorga. I show him the typewritten authorization, with its signature and official stamp. Dr Astorga tells me he has a lot of patients to see just now, that things will be quieter on Monday morning and that he may be able to talk to me then.

I come back on Monday morning to find that Dr Astorga's office is closed and the waiting room is empty. When I ask at reception I am informed: 'Dr Astorga doesn't work on Monday mornings.'

* * *

Emilio Alave began working in the mine when he was ten. Now, at the age of fifty, he smiles and – 'out of respect for my fellow miners' – refuses to comment on the newspaper rumours about the scale of his fortune: six, seven, eight million dollars.

He tells me that by the age of sixteen he was working forty-eight hours back to back, bringing out trucks full of ore without stopping to eat or sleep, only able to keep going by chewing coca leaves. When he was twenty-one he inherited a small find from his father, but for years it scarcely produced any ore, no matter how much he drilled, how hard he worked. At times, he went hungry and was on the verge of destitution. The only reason he refused to give up was because his father had told him the deposit would make him a millionaire. He turned to the Tío, the spirit who dwells in the bowels of the earth, made offerings to him and finally, at the age of thirty-two, a dynamite blast uncovered a rich seam of silver.

According to Alave, the only thing that differentiated him from other miners was the fact that, instead of squandering his earnings 'on drink and women', he reinvested the money. Now he is in charge of a number of companies which export tens of millions of dollars' worth of ore every year. He is president of the Compotosí cooperative, which has 450 members and employs another 2,500 casual workers. And he also owns transport companies, a soft drinks company, property investments, a hotel … and even a football team that bore his name when it competed in the second division of the Bolivian league. Atlético Nacional Emilio Alave changed its name to Nacional Potosí when the club won promotion. Alave travels around distributing gifts, he awards student grants to young people and he established a football school where Potosí's rising stars are educated for free. He used to be a centre-half for Compotosí, the team that won the mining cooperatives' league in 2009. According to journalist María José Vargas, Alave took to the pitch wearing a gold Rolex worth 49,000 dollars.

* * *

At one of the deposits worked by Compotosí, a labourer called Ricardo tells me that Emilio Alave never enters the mine, and that the workers know the reason why. I'm struggling to see the mystery: a man who has suffered two decades of hardship and poverty before striking it rich is hardly likely to want to go back below ground. But that's not why, Ricardo tells me, that's not the real reason. According to custom, a miner who has just made a find will often sacrifice a few llamas and sprinkle their blood at the entrance to the mine to ask Pachamama to guarantee the fertility of the minerals hidden in the rock. But Alave went further. He sacrificed one of his children. And buried the body in the mine. Pachamama responded to such a huge sacrifice with a huge reward: a rich seam of silver. That's why he became a millionaire, says Ricardo. But now, whenever he approaches the mine entrance, he hears the cries of his dead son from beneath the mountain. That's why Alave never enters the mine, Ricardo says, and the story travels by word of mouth below the ground.

* * *

Emilio Alave has a nephew, Richard Alave, who is also a mining entrepreneur, a member of the Compotosí cooperative and president of the Federation of Mining Cooperatives of Potosí (Fedecomin). He also runs a football team: Stormers San Lorenzo, who play in the second division.

Richard Alave is a powerful man: he can paralyse the whole of Potosí with a single speech.

One day, he gets up and calls on thousands of miners to march from Cerro Rico into the centre of Potosí, letting off dynamite as they go, to protest against the government.

They're demonstrating because the government is seeking to apply value-added tax to the mining cooperatives, a decision no president has dared to implement since 1987. The government doesn't actually want to collect any tax from the cooperatives; it just wants to apply the zero rate that exists under the law so that the government knows how much ore the cooperatives are really producing. Because the factories that process the ore and the companies that export it are in the habit of under-declaring the true quantities, to reduce their tax liabilities.

Richard Alave is preaching the apocalypse. Applying VAT regulations to the cooperatives will ruin them and throw thousands of miners out of work, he says, and the story travels by word of mouth below the ground.

* * *

'Emergency call for action. All members, delegates and workers in general are called to march for action. Assemble at 8.30 a.m. at the cooperative offices to protest against VAT. Attendance will be noted. The mines will be closed. The management.'

The message is written in chalk on a blackboard at the entrance to the Unified Mining Cooperative of Potosí, in the upper reaches of the mining district.

The morning is clear and cold. The miners are wearing helmets, boots and jackets. There are thousands of them. They fill the streets, tailing all the way back up the hill towards Cerro Rico, gathering in small groups, smoking, chatting, waiting for the demonstration to start.

At twenty to nine, a van with loudspeakers slowly sets off downhill.

'Let's go, comrades!'

The flag-bearer takes the first step. He's a veteran, about sixty years old. Messy locks of white hair poke out from beneath his helmet. He stares into the distance, his lips pressed together. He's carrying a large, diamond-shaped standard which is fixed to a wooden cross. It has the colours of the Bolivian national flag and bears an embroidered inscription: 'Departmental Federation of Mining Cooperatives of Potosí. Fedecomin. Founded 1 May 1955.' Behind the standard walk four women, wearing traditional coloured skirts, shawls over their shoulders and bowler hats on their heads. They carry a large green banner with yellow lettering: 'Fedecomin Potosí: Solidarity!'

They are followed by thousands of miners, grouped behind the banners of the individual cooperatives that make up the federation. Some of them walk in tight groups, others in long, martial lines: silent, serious, marching in step. They come down Calle Hernández, the main street of the mining district, towards the city centre, watched apprehensively by the local residents who crowd the pavements. The demonstrators carry handwritten placards: 'Death to VAT for the Mining Co-ops'. 'Down with the Hunger Tax of the Dictatorial Government of Evo Morales'. 'Death to the Ungrateful Government of Evo Morales'. 'We Demand our Fair Rights to the Cerro'. 'The Co-ops won't be Tricked by the Government'.

The march encounters a group of French tourists kitted out with helmets, overalls, boots, bags of coca leaves and bottles of liquor, on their way to a guided tour of the mine (the coca and liquor are for the miners). The guide tells me they are going to Pailaviri but he doesn't think they'll be able to make it up there today. They certainly won't. Every mine on Cerro Rico is deserted, and the miners have parked lorries across the roads to ensure that no vehicles can get through.

One of the tourists takes a photo of the march, smiles at the miners and gives them a thumbs-up.

The street is a succession of shops selling mining supplies; the attendants stand at the door – surrounded by drills, picks, bits, bolts, lamps, mallets, masks, helmets, overalls and boots – and watch the march go by. On the pavement is a woman in an apron and a hat, sitting on a stool behind a box draped with pink cloth, with a gas cylinder and a pan full of hot oil on a portable ring. She is preparing *rellenos de papa* – little fried balls of mashed potato stuffed with spicy mince and coated with egg and flour. Every few yards, there is a woman cooking: lentil rissoles, chips, savoury pastries, bowls of rice with meat.

Farther down, the march halts at a crossroads. The demonstration has become entangled with the traffic, a mixture of private cars and of the minibuses that are the city's public transport system. The air is filled with the sound of car horns and shouting. From the van leading the march, the loudspeakers announce:

'Comrades! Bus drivers! Understand our position! We are demonstrating to protect our jobs in Potosí!'

Suddenly, lots of the miners cover their ears with their hands ...

... a few seconds later, there is a string of explosions. The miners have thrown sticks of dynamite. Dogs flee, small children burst out crying, some of the spectators applaud, and the miners shout with joy.

They continue towards their final destination: the seat of the provincial government. They plan to occupy the Hall of Mirrors.

* * *

Two days later, there is fresh writing on the blackboard outside the Unified Mining Cooperative of Potosí: a list of the shifts for miners from each cooperative to block the four roads out of the city and the dirt tracks that go up to the mines.

I walk out of the city towards National Route 1. The junction is blocked by a barrier of boulders and several lorries. About a hundred men are sitting on the ground, chatting, dozing, listening to music. Some of the younger ones are playing football on the tarmac. On the verges, women in bowler hats and skirts, helped by their children, set up food stalls with gas rings, pots and plates, mashed potato and meat stuffing ready to fry, boxes containing soft drinks and bread rolls, bags of coca leaves, sweets, chocolate bars and chewing gum.

A wave of men and women are leaving the city, dragging suitcases, carrying babies in blankets, older children walking alongside. They are leaving Potosí on foot because they need to travel to other cities and they've been told that the buses are waiting a mile or so beyond the barriers, out of the range of the miners' stones.

The information is unclear. Somebody tells somebody else that they've heard that the bus for Tarija is waiting for passengers on Route 1, fifteen or twenty minutes' walk away. The passengers pass the blockade, dragging their suitcases in silence ...

(Except for one, who shouts something I don't understand. One of the miners shouts back: 'I'll kick your potato-faced, monkey-fucking ass!' But the tone is jokey rather than threatening.)

... and continue down the road. Some young men with motorbikes have spotted a business opportunity, shuttling back and forth, ferrying the travellers and their belongings to the waiting buses in exchange for a few pesos.

I walk back to Plaza 10 de Noviembre, in the centre of Potosí. The locals are gathered in groups on the benches and on the terraces of the cafés, complaining with suppressed anger about a blockade that has already been going on for two days. 'The prices in the supermarkets are going up,' says one. No supplies are getting through, there's a danger of shortages. Standing at the bar in a café, an old man relays the news of the helicopter. 'Haven't you heard about the helicopter?' And everyone listens to him. Some gringo tourists hired a helicopter this morning because they couldn't leave the city and they needed to get to La Paz to catch a flight back to their home country. The miners turned up, throwing stones, and the gringos couldn't take off. 'They're savages!' someone says. 'People are organizing convoys of cars out of the city by night, over the mountain tracks,' says another. And the police? They don't even dare go near the blockades.

Meanwhile, twenty or thirty miners have installed themselves in the Hall of Mirrors in the provincial government building. At the end of the demonstration they occupied the hall and issued a communiqué: they wouldn't move or lift the blockade until the minister of the economy and the minister for regions travelled to Potosí to guarantee, in person, that the VAT law would not be applied (not even with a zero rating), that the government would draft a special law for the Potosí cooperatives, and that the co-ops would be allowed to continue working above an altitude of 4,400 metres – the height above which Comibol cancelled mining concessions to prevent the mountain from collapsing.

The ministers aren't coming, but today a central government representative is flying in from La Paz to agree to the mining cooperatives' demand for a special law.

The next day's newspapers all have the same photo on the front page: Richard Alave, in a blue tracksuit with an orange helmet, shaking the hand of Susana Ríos, deputy minister for tax policy, after signing a memorandum of understanding. Ríos is smiling, but not as much as Alave.

* * *

I ask the Federation of Cooperatives for an interview with Richard Alave and the secretary tells me to come back the next day, at three in the afternoon.

I arrive at five to three and I'm shown into a waiting room, the anteroom to Alave's office. The secretary – in a blue skirt suit, her eyes framed by butterfly glasses, a disapproving look on her face – is working at a desk at the far end of the room. Eight men sit waiting on sofas. Three of them are dressed smartly, in shirts and ties, and are checking something on a laptop. Two more wear tracksuits and pass the time flicking through a newspaper without actually reading any of the articles, or staring at the floor, bored. The other three, in jeans and coats, are looking through masses of paperwork in various folders. My arrival is acknowledged with a nod and I take a seat in a free armchair. After a while, one of the men in track-suits passes me the newspaper, in case I want to read it. He looks as if he's been waiting for a long time. When he asks the secretary how things are going, she answers curtly:

'Mr Alave doesn't have a timetable.'

The tracksuited man whispers to me that he had an appointment for two thirty. It's now half past three.

On the door to the office hangs a sign: 'Mr Alave is unable to accept honorary godfather nominations.' It is customary to name important people as godfathers so that they will pay for parties, processions and other costly events.

A tall, slender, white-haired woman comes into the room and explains her problem to the secretary. The day the miners marched down into town, a dynamite blast broke the window of an elderly neighbour. A representa-tive of the federation took a note of the neighbour's name and address, and promised to pay for the repair. The secre-tary searches for a document with the details.

'Well, there's nothing here.'

The white-haired woman protests, asks her to look properly, repeats her story. The dynamite went off, the window broke, it was a pane of glass this size, the man said the federation would pay for the repairs.

'I can't do anything. There's nothing here. Tell your neighbour to come in if she wants to make a claim.'

'But I've already told you she's very old, she can't come.'

'I'm sorry but there's nothing I can do about it. Others have already been paid because their details were here. Look …' and she waves a piece of paper in the air.

'But that can't be right. Who's in charge here?'

'Mr Alave.'

'Is that his office?'

'Yes.'

'Is he coming out?'

'At some point.'

'Well, I'm going to wait for him.'

'I can't say how long he'll be, madam.'

The woman reluctantly takes a seat on one of the sofas, next to the tracksuited men.

Whenever the secretary looks up from her papers and glances vaguely in my direction, I try my hardest to make eye contact. At quarter to four, with no news of President Alave, the secretary goes out into the corridor, knocks on the door of another office, opens it, sticks her head in, talks for a moment, then comes to find me. She tells me that Guillermo Condori Ramos, chair of the Audit Committee, can see me.

I go through. Condori is tall, well built with wide shoulders, abundant wavy grey hair, a droopy white moustache. He is sixty-three years old and is one of the historic leaders of the cooperative movement.

'I'm alive and healthy because I was a leader from early on. I went down the mine as a lad but I didn't stay there for long. Otherwise, I'd have been six foot underground by the age of forty, like my dad, like most of my fellow miners.'

His career is sprinkled with capital letters. He's a member of the Villa Imperial Mining Cooperative and chair of the Audit Committee of the Federation of Mining Cooperatives of Potosí, responsible for checking the accounts and ensuring that everything is above board. Before that, from the mid-1980s onwards, he served several terms as president and deputy president of the federation. And he was a member of the Bolivian parliament, representing the Revolutionary Nationalist Movement, the party of Víctor Paz Estenssoro, the party that nationalized the mines following the revolution of 1952, the same one that dismantled the state-owned mining sector in 1986.

Condori tells me the cooperatives had to buy Comibol's clapped-out equipment, that the deposits are almost exhausted, the work is very hard, the profits low. Even so, they generate wealth because they create jobs, they pay the state for the mining leases, mineral duties, social security contributions. And that's enough. Special activity deserves special treatment.

'VAT exemption is a progressive measure,' he says.

The cooperatives are also exempt from paying other taxes that apply to the rest of the industry. In 2012, they paid a mere 5 per cent of the value of their output in taxes, according to a report by the Bolivia Documentation and Information Centre (CEDIB), while the figure paid by private companies was around 67 per cent, according to the Pazos Kanki Foundation. What's more, the cooperatives receive state loans on favourable terms, their applications for new concessions go through on a nod and a wink, they ignore environmental and employment legislation, and they sublet their contracts to multinationals and bank huge profits that end up in the pockets of 'a group of cooperative members that operates as an elite', according to CEDIB. The government of Evo Morales turned a blind eye for ten years because it didn't want to antagonize such a large sector of society and one that is able to bring the country to a standstill with its protests (100,000 co-op members plus their families represent half a million votes).

'Some leaders have used the legal advantages of the cooperatives to make a lot of money,' I suggest to Condori.

'A lot of people risked their money, their time, their health, and they failed. They spent their whole lives working and ended up poor. Others got rich in a day. That's mining! And if a miner has taken risks, has worked for years without making a peso, has lived in poverty and nobody has helped him, and then one day he strikes silver, well, good luck to him. But instead he gets called a capitalist, a millionaire. The way I see it, he's taken a risk and it's paid off.'

'But what about the *peones*, the casual labourers, working without contracts, for low wages, without safety equipment ...'

'First of all, there are no *peones* any more.'

'Really?'

'We call them associate members. We can't have them on the payroll. They don't work full eight-hour shifts because the areas of the mine where they work are too dangerous. Sometimes they're only in the mine for three or four hours so we can't pay them the minimum wage. They're not regular workers. Most of them are peasants who work seasonally: before the harvest, after the harvest.

They work for a few weeks and then, whenever they want to, they leave. We could offer them contracts, with deductions for social security payments and medical insurance, but they're the ones who don't want it.'

'But isn't it compulsory?'

'They just want to make as much money as they can and then go back to their villages. They come and go. We can't give them permanent contracts.'

'But the guards and the *palliris* live up on the mountain. They never leave but they don't have contracts or insurance either.'

'But it's the same with them! When they want to, those women just up sticks and leave. They're unreliable. How can we give them a contract? Some of them get the minimum wage. Others are paid less but have the right to work the leftover rock, and they make a lot of money from that. Sometimes they make more than the members! They're no fools: they smuggle out the best ore, mixed with other rock so it won't be noticed, and they make a good profit. But they also rob each other. And they allow the tools to be stolen. They complain but some of them earn more than the co-op members. The members invest, they open up a find, they run the risk that it might not be productive. And then the casual labourers and the guards, who don't risk their money, want to earn the same. It's not right.'

'And what about their children? There are kids working in the cooperative mines.'

'Look. When we were kids, we used to go up to the *canchamina* too. We took food for our parents. My dad was a miner, my mum was a *palliri*. We were up there with them. We played. But we weren't going to spend the whole day doing nothing. So we helped out. The kids, once they're there, they lend a hand with the work.'

* * *

In 2014, the Potosí Public Prosecutor's office interviewed 140 adolescent workers who lived on the slopes of Cerro Rico (112 of them worked inside the mine, 28 outside). It presented the following statistics:

Ninety-five per cent of them had no written contract; 42 per cent didn't know who they were working for, while the remaining 58 per cent worked for cooperative members or for casual labourers.

They earned an average of 2,400 pesos a month (slightly less than 400 dollars) for four hours a day: a high salary in Bolivia.

Eighty-four per cent had no health insurance – if they got ill or suffered an accident they had to pay for any health treatment they received, or they used traditional remedies; 94 per cent had received no safety training, 84 per cent didn't have any safety gear, and the other 16 per cent paid for it out of their own pockets.

Sixty-four per cent didn't go to school; 74 per cent would have preferred to work in another industry; 94 per cent were unaware of their rights and didn't know who to turn to for help.

The report also offered some conclusions. The cooperatives didn't provide decent employment for their workers, and even less so for adolescents; they didn't invest in safety, provide health insurance or respect employment law; the state had no presence on Cerro Rico, failing to regulate or monitor employment conditions or to protect the human rights of those who lived there – people who lacked health services, decent housing, sewage systems, drinking water, clean air or protection from violence, in a place where aggression, robbery and sexual assault were commonplace.

* * *

On 25 August 2016, a group of cooperative members kidnapped Rodolfo Illanes, deputy minister for security.

It was a show of strength, because Evo Morales' government had finally plucked up the courage to exert its control over the cooperatives. It had announced a law to extend employment rights to the sector's 100,000 casual workers, granting them the right to join trade unions (something which had previously been denied) and requiring them to be registered with the social security, health and pension contribution systems, like any other Bolivian worker. The cooperative leaders rebelled against the reforms. Five thousand miners were sent out to block roads across the country; they hurled dynamite at police officers who had been sent to dislodge them, and they threatened to occupy a number of city centres. Then they imposed a set of conditions that would have to be met if they were to remove the blockades: the government would have to withdraw the recognition of employment rights, stop attempting to enforce environmental standards, and grant them new concessions.

One of the blockades cut Bolivia's main highway, the route that joins La Paz, Oruro and Potosí, and Deputy Minister Illanes went to negotiate with the demonstrators on behalf of the government. The miners took him hostage. The police charged the demonstrators and there was a pitched battle, with bullets and dynamite. A miner, Rubén Aparaya, was killed by a police bullet. When the kidnappers heard the news, they forced the deputy minister to walk barefoot up the mountain, beat him, forced him to continue walking on his knees, threw him down the hill, hurled stones at him, broke his ribs, his arms and his legs, and crushed his head with a rock. They wrapped the body in a sheet and left it in the road.

By the time the clashes were over, three more miners had been killed by police bullets, another had died when a stick of dynamite exploded in his hand, twenty-seven people were injured, and dozens were arrested.

In Bolivia, public opinion hardened against the cooperative leaders, against their abuses and their privileges. The government decided not only to push ahead with its employment reform in the mining industry but to promote new laws: the cooperatives would have to pay VAT, submit to audits and give up any deposits they had subleased to multinationals. Any co-ops that failed to observe the principles of the cooperative movement would have to operate as private companies.

* * *

Alicia has to go into town tomorrow to pick up a uniform. She's happy, but also slightly nervous and impatient.

She says she's going to finish high school at the very least. But she also wants to find another job. A few days ago she went to the barracks to submit her grades and have a medical check-up, and now her uniform is waiting for her.

We're in the courtyard of a cluster of buildings in the mining district of Potosí. It's the home of Fundación Voces Libres, a Swiss NGO that helps the children who work in the mines, and their families. Today is Sunday, and they've organized a day of games, followed by a rather unusual theatre performance, but the woman who's going to direct the show hasn't arrived from La Paz. They tell us her bus is late because there's been an accident or a traffic jam.

While we're waiting, they show us the dressmaking and carpentry workshops, the classrooms, the radio station where some of the kids get hands-on experience, the apartments where women and children who have suffered the worst cases of violence can seek refuge.

'Mercedes is here!'

5

The Devil

Mercedes Cortez sweeps into the hall like a hurricane. She runs around, greets people, laughs, shakes hands, grabs the microphone, takes a breath and talks to the 200 people who have gathered to listen to her. The children are sitting on the floor, the mothers are on chairs while, standing at the back of the hall, are the unlikely protagonists of this event: thirty miners, thirty fathers.

The mothers are frequent visitors to the foundation. For almost all of the fathers, this is their first time: they have been expressly invited and have been promised a gift.

Mercedes – in her late twenties, tall, dark-skinned, wearing a long grey coat and a cream headscarf – moves from one side of the hall to the other, mic in hand, encouraging the audience to join in. The children and the mums sing along, laughing and dancing. The dads look on, seriously.

'Let's say a special hello to all the dads who are here with us today. It's very important that they're here because today we're going to talk about kindness. We're going to give the dads a card with ten golden rules. And we're going to give them a special vaccine: the "anti-whack vac". What do you think it's for?'

'So they don't hit us!' shout the kids.

'That's right! But this isn't just about telling people off. Today we're also going to be giving out presents. We're going to give a football to every dad who is brave enough to come up after the performance to tell us about what kindness means for him. But first, it's theatre time!'

Mercedes asks for volunteers. Half a dozen kids come up and act out typical scenes from home. Guadalupe – five or six years old – has got dirty playing in the mud and Mercedes acts the part of her mum, shouting at her, insulting her, belittling her. Then she turns to the audience.

'Kids. How does Guadalupe feel now?'

'Saaaaaaad!'

Mercedes explains that loving words are very important: that you don't buy them at the market, they don't cost anything to use, it's just as easy to be kind as to be cruel. She repeats the scene with Guadalupe, but this time with kindness.

More scenes follow: arguments between mum and dad, a drunk dad who pushes his wife and kids … The children recognize the scenes instantly, they follow them, interpret them, complete the dialogues, the arguments. At the end, Mercedes talks about psychological abuse, about the long-term trauma caused by violence and cruelty, about how mums and dads need to look after their children, how children have the right to play, to get messy, to be naughty, because they're children, they're exploring the world, they're learning, and they should never be subjected to violence. She talks about the benefits of bringing up children with kindness.

And about the need to respect children's bodies. No adult should use children's bodies. It's really important to be aware of sexual abuse, to make sure it never happens.

'Kids, do any of you have bumps or bruises?'

Several kids raise their hands or point at each other. They know which of their friends have been hit recently. A lively kid, three or four years old, his face half covered by his sweatshirt hood, gets up and skips towards Mercedes. She bends down, looks at him closely, removes the hood and strokes his hair. The boy has a black eye.

'What happened to you, dear?'

The boy is silent.

Mercedes strokes his hair again. And he answers in a quiet voice.

'I fell.'

Another slightly older boy comes up, eight or nine years old. He lifts up his shirt to reveal a mass of bruises. He's been given a real beating.

'Who did this to you, darling?'

'My uncle.'

'Why did he hit you?'

'Because I made him angry.'

'Really? What did you do?'

'I lost my keys.'

The kids return to their seats and Mercedes reads out the card with the ten golden rules of kindness: I will hug you every day and tell you I love you; instead of shouting at you, I will listen to you; I won't make you do heavy chores; I will spend my free time with you instead of getting drunk with my friends ... She also holds up a poster for the mums to take home and hang on the wall. It shows two dads: a monstrous one hitting his family and shouting at them, and a heroic one playing with his kids and listening to them.

'Now let's encourage the dads to come out and tell us what they think about kindness.'

The women and children turn to look at the men at the back of the hall. The miners nervously make their way to the front and approach Mercedes. The first to dare take the mic is a young man with a baseball cap and a moustache, who stares at the floor as he talks.

'We have to encourage the *wawas* to tell us their problems. We should never hit them or pinch them.'

One by one, the rest follow. Each says a sentence then passes the mic on, and Mercedes' assistants give them a football and a copy of the card.

'We should hold our *wawas*' hands on the way to school.'

'We shouldn't drink so much, we shouldn't come home drunk.'

'We shouldn't ask our kids to do heavy chores.'

* * *

There are three teachers: María, María and María. They allow me to accompany them but don't want me to publish their real names, they don't want to call attention to what they're doing, don't want anyone to know that they are telling people about it.

This week, the miners have organized more blockades and the school bus can't make it up the track to the Cerro Rico. So the teachers go up on foot and collect children from their houses. We come to a low brick house, a bit more solid than Alicia's hut, on a *canchamina*.

'Miguelito! It's time to come and learn to read and write!'

The three teachers never go up the mountain on their own.

'Miguelito!'

A woman comes out. She's about forty, wearing skirts, an apron and a woolly hat. She is followed by a four-year-old boy in a blue tracksuit and a yellow hat, who runs towards the teachers, skipping and flapping his arms. A teenage girl watches us silently from the window. One of the teachers goes up to the window, talks to her for a moment and then says goodbye.

We continue uphill until we reach a small white building, surrounded by a brick boundary wall to protect it from the wind and the dust. It was built by Cepromin and must be a candidate for the highest school in the world. It serves the children of mining families but it isn't an official school. The kids get support classes, help with their homework, therapy, food, a hot shower. Nestling on this rocky slope, 4,500 metres up, among craters and pyramids of slag, it looks like a moon base.

'The girl in the window is Carmencita,' one of the Marías says. 'She's Miguelito's sister. She never leaves the house if she sees strangers. She was raped by a miner, became pregnant and gave up school because she was ashamed. She gave birth at home, right here, and the birth was very difficult. She really suffered. And now she just stays home, looking after her *wawa*.'

'How old is she?'

'Fourteen.'

The teacher says that Carmencita was very good at school. Clever, hard-working, she wanted to study, to get a job, to live in town. Until she was raped and she stopped going out.

Cepromin fought hard. Its director, Cecilia Molina, found a lawyer for Carmencita, they reported the attack, wrote letters to the minister of justice to ask her to deal with the case, urged her to stop ignoring the issue of rape in the mines. Sexual crimes are so frequent, so widely accepted even in the victims' own families, that nobody is surprised, nobody ever reports them, nobody expects anything to be done.

Cepromin succeeded in bringing the first ever case for rape on Cerro Rico. The judge found the accused guilty and sent him to prison. But he was freed after three months, with the agreement of Carmencita's family. The rapist apologized and agreed to give them money to help pay for the baby.

> It was terrible. They agreed out of fear. Carmencita's father is a mine security guard, working for the same cooperative as the man who raped his daughter. And the miners threatened him. They said he'd lose his job, that they were going to beat him up, and one day they told him they would kill him if he didn't take back the accusation. So he asked us to withdraw the case. He came to the Cepromin office and begged us. He was terrified. He said they had put the evil eye on him, performed witchcraft, and that he couldn't sleep and was ill. Eventually, the rapist's lawyer offered a deal and Carmencita's father accepted. It's awful. How can there be reconciliation between a rapist and his victim when the victim is a thirteen-year-old girl? What kind of a deal is that?

María explains that it was very important to finally apply the law. Important to try the accused, to find him guilty, to protect the girl and her family, to put an end to impunity.

'Miners have this idea that they can abuse women whenever they want. They go out and get drunk and think that gives them licence to do whatever they feel like. That's the way it's always been. Everyone says: "you know, that's how miners are". If they don't do anything too serious – if the girl doesn't get badly beaten or killed – then nothing happens. Sexual abuse has never been punished because the police never come up here, to the mines. Cerro Rico is a no-go area for the law.'

*   *   *

A dozen or so adolescent girls with serious expressions are waiting in a room. They are well wrapped up – in coats, thick jumpers, scarves, shawls and woollen hats – and barely exchange a word. They're here for a sex education workshop. The atmosphere is far more tense than in the other classrooms.

The teachers tell me that, obviously, I can't attend. Almost all these girls have suffered abuse at the hands of a family member: a cousin, an uncle, their father. It's tradition. Even their own mothers often tell their daughters not to make a big deal out of it. You know what men are like. Three of the girls have been attacked by strangers. I ask what they mean by 'attacked' and they say harassment, assault, rape. The teachers are also worried about another four or five girls who are around fifteen years old and go to the bars in the mining district, where the men buy them drinks, give them presents, offer them money and sleep with them. The teachers talk to them about their sexual rights, explain that nobody can force them to do something they don't want to do, that they don't have to let their uncle or their father get into bed with them and touch them, that they have the right to refuse when one of the miners gives them a teddy bear or a keyring, buys them a few beers and then says, 'get into my car, I'll give you a lift', 'you're looking sexy, let's go somewhere quiet'. Sometimes horrible things happen to the girls and they don't want to tell anyone.

'We have to break this cycle of mothers telling their daughters that these things happen, that there's no point making a fuss or complaining. When we talk to the next generation, we say that if something happens to them, if they're afraid or unsure, then they should tell us.'

The teachers are also afraid. Some of the miners keep an eye on them.

'They know who we are. Sometimes one of the miners is involved with our girls; sometimes they come and insult us. That's why we never go up the mountain alone. We always go in pairs or as a group of three, because the miners come and chase us, they follow us, threatening us and laughing at us.'

They say it's important to educate the girls, but what's more important – more difficult – is educating the boys.

'We thought about going at night and putting up posters at the mine entrances so the miners would see them in the morning. We wanted to write that violence against women is a crime, that the perpetrators can go to prison, just that. That women have the right to say no, and men have to respect them.'

'We also thought that maybe we should organize a meeting with the miners, go up to the mine, give a speech about these issues.'

'But we're still too afraid.'

* * *

While they're leading their workshop, I sit in an empty classroom and copy my notes onto my laptop. After a while, a boy comes in and sits at another desk.

Johnny Oquendo is fifteen and struggles to write simple sentences. He asks me to help him with his homework, an essay about the work he's done at the Cepromin centre. Along with some other boys, Johnny cleared a plot next to the school, and they built a hut and painted it in bright colours to create a playhouse for the younger children. But now he has to write about it and he's really struggling.

Johnny is tall and gangling, and looks slightly fragile. His short fringe falls diagonally across his forehead, covering his left eye, masking his shy gaze. He talks softly, in a voice that is scarcely audible but which becomes slightly louder when we go outside and he proudly shows me his work. The playhouse is a recycled fibreglass water tank, which he has painted with windows and flowers and into which he has cut a door.

He says he can show me the Cerro if I want. He'd like to be a tourist guide. He knows spots where I can take nice photos.

First, he takes me to the loading dock. At the top, rails lead from the mine entrance. Two miners have pushed a truck along the rails, and now they're tipping its contents onto a scree-covered slope. At the bottom of each dock is a set of floodgates, which can be opened to allow the mineral-rich rock to pour out into the lorries waiting below.

What Johnny notices most are the cracks and craters. We are near the top of Cerro Rico, the part where the risk of collapse is at its highest. The mountain is like a crumbling sandcastle and it feels as if, with every step we take, the earth is going to swallow us up. One of the holes – four or five metres wide, three metres deep – has taken a huge chunk out of the road. The pickups can get past but the lorries can't.

'This is new. One day it wasn't there and the next day it had just appeared.'

We scramble over the slope because Johnny wants to show me a panoramic view of Potosí. From up here we can make out the baroque old town – the cathedral, the mansion roofs, the convent courtyards, the church towers. Around it sprawl barrios of tightly-packed low houses, long narrow roads, two football stadiums, not a single green space; on the outskirts are shanty towns, the low rays of the evening sun glinting on the zinc roofs of makeshift huts.

Johnny points out a mine entrance a little higher up the slope behind us.

'Have you ever been down the mine?' he asks.

'Yes.'

'I don't like it. I don't want to work in the mines.'

Sitting on the hill, Johnny produces his sentences one by one, as if they are stones that he must first cough up from his stomach and then spit out through his mouth.

He looks at the ground as he talks, occasionally picking a pebble from the hillside and throwing it into the air.

'My friends have been working in the mine since they were small. Some of them began when they were twelve. Pushing trucks.'

'And how are they?'

'They're happy because they make money. But they're always tired.'

He talks then falls silent and throws another pebble.

'Some of them died in rockfalls.'

'Friends of yours?'

'A cousin.'

He throws another pebble.

'Do they ask you if you want to work there? Do they offer you work?'

'Yes. My friends are always telling me I should go to the mine to make some money. But I want to study. I want to be a doctor. Or a lawyer.'

'What would you most like to be?'

'I'd like to learn English to become an astronaut.' He smiles. 'Or to be a guide. I want to go down the mine – but just to take tourists. We get lots of tourists. Spanish, French, American. I want to take them on guided tours of the mine.'

'Can you make a lot of money from tourists?'

'I think so. But I don't want to work in the mine. I know – if I start now – by the time I'm twenty-five I'll have silicosis.'

Johnny was born in the Siglo XX miners' camp in Lla-llagua. His father was a driller, but he lost his job and the whole family moved to Potosí a few years ago.

'Drilling is the worst job because you're always breathing clouds of dust. Now my dad has miner's disease. And he's paralysed; he can't move half of his body. He just spends his time in bed watching TV.'

He can't go to hospital because he doesn't have any medical insurance. And at home things aren't good, says Johnny, because the house is tiny and only has an earth floor. It's very cold.

'What's your dad like?'

Johnny throws another pebble down the hill.

'Miners drink a lot. They're violent. My dad used to beat my mum, really bad. Then, when we got bigger, me and my brothers stopped him.'

Johnny has a recurring nightmare in which he sees his father's huge hands, just the hands, the hands of a driller, hitting him.

'He used to hit me hard, until I was ten. After that, he couldn't. But it's affected me. My head isn't right.'

* * *

I go to Johnny's house a couple of days later. Doctor Eduardo, on his rounds visiting the sick, is manoeuvring his four-wheel-drive along the winding tracks of Cerro Rico. He works for Cepromin and is accompanied by the organization's director, Cecilia Molina, and by me.

'Johnny's dad – Ramiro – is awful,' says Cecilia.

Ramiro worked in the Llallagua mines and married a local woman. But he was also in the habit of raping two of his cousins: Luisa and Elsa. When he got Elsa pregnant, he abandoned his wife and went to live with Elsa. Johnny was the result of that pregnancy.

Shortly afterwards, Ramiro was dismissed from the mine ...

'Because he's completely useless, he's lazy and he's violent.'

... and the family moved from Llallagua to Potosí. They had four more children. Ramiro worked as a security guard for a cooperative on Cerro Rico for ten years, guarding the mine entrance, but he lost that job too: he was always drunk, he disappeared, he was completely unreliable.

And when they threw him out of his job, they also threw him out of the adobe hut on the *canchamina* where he lived with Elsa and their five young children. There was only one person they could turn to for help: Luisa, the other cousin that Ramiro used to rape in Llallagua. She had moved to Cerro Rico with another miner, and the couple already had five children.

'Imagine,' says Cecilia. 'Two couples and their ten children in a two-room brick house. Everyone slept in two big beds.'

As we round the curve, the house appears, sitting among heaps of mining spoil. It's made of brick, painted pumpkin yellow, and covered with corrugated iron, held in place by piles of rocks. There is also a TV aerial, and a cable brings electricity from the pylons that supply the mines. It's surrounded by debris: the rusting chassis of an abandoned car, plastic water drums, mattresses with the stuffing spilling out, old tyres, cardboard boxes, planks, broken bricks, a few toys. Two dogs run among the rubbish.

Leaning against the back of the house is a miserable hut, although really it's more like an igloo made from piles of stone, wrapped in plastic, with sheets of grimy canvas covering the gaps. It's a metre and a half high and no more than fifteen metres square.

'They live there now,' explains Cecilia. 'Ramiro built the hut to have somewhere to live with Elsa and the five kids, so they could move out of Luisa's house.'

Doctor Eduardo parks twenty metres from the stone igloo.

'Ramiro's bone idle,' says Cecilia, before she gets out of the vehicle. 'We offered to help him build a brick house, we were prepared to pay half the cost of the materials but he didn't want to. He said that adobe was enough. He didn't even make the adobe blocks: one day it was raining and they wouldn't dry properly, the next day he was tired … he just piled up these stones instead. Now he's ill and he hardly moves. At least he can't beat his wife or abuse his daughters or his nieces. When they were eight years old, he showed them porn films to get them ready. Then he abused them.'

Elsa – Johnny's mother – comes out of the brick house. She's breastfeeding a three-month-old baby, her fifth child, the dying miner's last. Behind her is Luisa, the other cousin, pregnant with her sixth child. Both women are stocky, their skin burned by the sun and the dust. Johnny isn't at home.

The doctor asks the women how Ramiro is doing.

'He's very sick,' Elsa replies. 'Before, he used to go out sometimes, he'd take a few steps and sit over there, on the rocks. But now he can't move his arm or his leg at all. He hasn't got out of bed for two weeks. I put a diaper on him but he gets angry and takes it off. It's impossible. He just soils himself.'

The doctor heads towards the stone igloo, lifts aside the sheet of metal that covers the doorway and goes into the gloom. Elsa follows him. The rest of us wait at the threshold. The smell is dense and fetid. When my eyes become accustomed to the dark, I make out a bed and the shape of the dying man between the sheets. I see Ramiro's puffy face, his hair plastered with sweat, his cheeks wet, his mouth set fast in panic. When he recognizes the doctor, Ramiro groans.

'I don't want to die, Doctor! Have pity on me!'

He lets out a long, high screech, until he runs out of breath and starts to cough. After an unbearable struggle, he finally fills his lungs with air, breathes again, sobs, then starts to cry softly.

From the threshold, I can see the hand that appears in Johnny's dreams, the huge hand of a driller, paralysed by stroke, hanging limp at one side of the bed, large, swollen, purple.

* * *

'We're always afraid,' says Johnny's mother, Elsa, as she sits on a rock breastfeeding her baby. 'We see it all, up here on the Cerro. Robberies, fights. Nobody protects us.'

'A few days ago, a peasant girl comes running up. Over there on the path, screaming,' says Luisa, Johnny's aunt. 'Sixteen or so, she'd be. She said she was being chased by some miners in a car, they wanted to kill her. "Run down the hill," I tell her, "run." Because up here on the Cerro, nobody will help you. They might kill you. If you're lucky, they'll just rape you.'

* * *

Alicia's mother, Rosa, spent a night in town, at her eldest daughter's house. She came back up the Cerro the next day, went inside, and realized that Alicia and Evelyn weren't there. On the table was a blood-smeared glass.

'My God! I was scared out of my mind.'

She ran off to look for Alicia and Evelyn, and found them in Lorena's house. They were safe but terrified.

'The blood wasn't ours,' Alicia explains. 'That night we were asleep and we heard the noise of a car approaching. It stopped and I was afraid so I got up. I heard some men shouting. They weren't there for long; they slammed the doors and drove off. So I went out and realized they'd thrown something onto the road. It was strange, like a huge white bag. I put on my helmet and went over with a torch to have a look.'

The bundle was a girl, fifteen or sixteen years old. They'd tied her up, wrapped her in one of the sacks they use for carrying ore, and dumped her on the mountain. She was almost completely naked, her hands and feet were tied, and her mouth was bleeding heavily. Several of her teeth were broken.

'I went back inside for a knife and I cut the ropes. Then I gave her a glass of water. She drank and left some blood on the glass; that's what my mum saw.'

Alicia ran to her aunt's house. They told the other guards, who went down to look after the girl. She said a man had given her a lift from the disco and then some other men had got into the car.

'She didn't say anything else. She was so frightened she couldn't speak.'

Some of the guards took the girl down the hill to the police post in the mining district. After that, the incident gradually faded from people's minds.

'A few days later, a woman came, the public prosecutor's assistant,' says Rosa,

and she asked us what had happened. We told her and she said we should go down into the town to give a statement. But we never went because two miners came to say they knew who we were, that we lived here, and that we shouldn't report anything. I think they were relatives of the men who'd attacked the girl. So we were afraid. Up here, we never see the police, we're alone. At night, the miners come with their cars, they get drunk, they crash their cars, get into fights. They come looking for girls. So we're scared. That's why we always have dogs, and sticks of dynamite ready, to defend ourselves if they come. If they come too close, we throw dynamite. A few days ago we were sleeping and a man came and started hammering on the door. He was really drunk. I phoned my sister and she came with some other women. They shouted at him, threw dynamite and the man left.

* * *

Adalberto Miranda points to the tower of the Church of the Conception, which is cracked and leans slightly to one side.

'It's about to go. The next rainy season, it's going to fall.'

Adalberto is one of those quiet, resigned men. He doesn't lose his temper; he's quite familiar with disasters, so much so that one might assume he accepts them. But he doesn't. Adalberto – with his sleepy eyes, bushy moustache, hands resting on his stomach – sits on a bench in the square and tells us to look at the little hospital next to the church, because at any moment a car with injured miners will pull up.

It's a clear calm evening and it's very pleasant, just sitting here in the sun.

I met Adalberto because Alicia wanted to talk to him and she allowed me to tag along. The three of us sit on the bench in the square, between the rickety church tower and the hospital where the injured miners will soon appear. Adalberto is president of the neighbourhood association of Concepción, a mining district in the highest part of Potosí, where the tarmac roads give way to the dirt tracks that lead up the mountain. Alicia is president of the assembly of child workers of the Cerro Rico, and she's suggested a plan for the local council to create jobs in the area for young people from mining families: cleaning the streets, maintaining the squares, looking after the parks in this neglected neighbourhood. Adalberto likes the idea. Alicia says that some young people want jobs like that but others prefer to work in the mine.

'Of course. Who wouldn't want to be a miner,' Adalberto says, 'when a furniture mover earns thirty pesos in eight hours and a miner can make three times that amount from pushing trucks for four hours. Miners make money. But they don't live beyond fifty.'

I ask Alicia if that's right, if kids really are attracted by the wages, given that she was paid only one fifth of what an adult would earn for the same work.

'It's different for the boys,' she says. 'When they're sixteen or eighteen, the cooperative starts to pay them more. Like an adult. They become assistant drillers and make a lot more.'

'Aren't they worried about how dangerous it is?'

'Well, they're proud of being miners. They want to be like their dads, to feel brave and strong. And earning money gives them authority at home.'

'And your brother?'

'Yes, he's a bit like that. He comes home and tells my mum to make food for him, to wash his clothes. He earns money and buys nice clothes, he goes out drinking with his mates, and when he comes home, he likes to boss people around. That's what miners are like. Sometimes I argue with him, but we still love each other.'

We've only been there for twenty minutes when a van pulls up and three men get out. One of them limps into the hospital, leaning on the shoulders of his companions.

'This is a quiet day,' says Adalberto. 'On a normal day you get eight or ten injured miners. They come in bleeding or unconscious, with crushed limbs or fractured skulls ... Every week, men in their twenties or thirties are killed, sometimes even kids of fifteen. Last month, we lost a young lad who lived in this street. He was going up a ladder in a shaft when a boulder fell on him and knocked him off. He fell several metres down to the bottom. His body was shattered.'

Adalberto seems calm and talks in a low voice but he is raging.

They're terrible. All they care about is making money.
Lots of them are peasants, they come for a season

and earn as much as they can, and they don't want medical insurance or anything else, they just want their wages in their pocket. They stick a few pieces of timber in the gallery and that's that, they go in without thinking about it. If they have a family, they don't spend the money on a decent house: they rent the cheapest place they can and cram themselves into a tiny hovel. The ones who earn a lot blow it all on four-wheel-drives. You've probably noticed them in the barrio. They bring them over from Japan, for thirty or forty thousand dollars. They have nowhere to live but they go crazy about a car. It's their awful pride. And their fatalism. They're incredibly fatalistic, but that's hardly a surprise: in the mine you can die at any moment so you take your money and you spend it on cars, drink, whores and parties. You've never been here for Carnival. They spend a fortune. They bring the best bands from La Paz, they go down to Potosí dressed up, dancing, drinking, having one long party. Every Friday they go out on a spree because that's the day they get paid. A gang of them go to a brothel, the place shuts its doors to everyone else, it's only open to the miners for the whole weekend. Then the pickpockets come to prey on the drunk miners, because they've always got lots of cash on them, and there are terrible fights. We stay at home. We tell the girls not to even think of going out alone on Friday and Saturday nights.

On Saturday, the miners' wives usually appear with their kids in tow, looking for their husbands in the bars. The women need money to buy food, and it always ends in shouting and brawling.

'That's a miner's life. Making money and drinking it away, making money and drinking it away, until you die.'

Miners have to stand drinks for their comrades when they get a big pay packet. It's money they've made thanks to the magical help of the Tío and they have to share it with their companions, they have to buy rounds of drinks, pay for parties, because if the Tío's wealth doesn't flow, he gets angry and sends misfortune. The seam runs out, the miner gets sick or somebody dies.

Adalberto tells about how a cousin of his made a lot of money in the mine, and bought three minibuses and set up a transport company. One of the buses went over the edge of a cliff and a passenger died. And everyone said it was a punishment, because he'd kept all the money for his business instead of celebrating with his comrades when he found the seam. Adalberto gives a faint smile.

'Fairy tales.'

Then he points out the cracked tower again, the road-sides overflowing with rubbish, the broken street lights.

All the money that comes out of the Cerro just gets spent on debauchery, on cars and nothing else. This city's dying. Look at the Pailaviri district. It used to have factories, houses, shops; it used to be full of life. Then the factory closed down and now there's nothing, just ruins. The miners don't contribute anything to the community. They exploit everything, they take everything and leave nothing. The only thing mining gives us is problems. We get violence, pollution, processing mills in the middle of the barrio, right next to our houses. When they process the ore, they emit clouds of dust, creating a poisonous fog.

The residents protest. They have headaches and breathing problems; the pollution makes them ill. They demand that the cooperatives build sheds to enclose the processing mills to contain the dust; they call for the cooperatives to cover the lorries and to spray to keep the dust down. But the cooperatives take no notice and nobody enforces the law.

'In Potosí, the only law is the law of the miners,' says Adalberto.

And when the mining finishes, the city will disappear. We've been living with the mine for five centuries and in all that time nothing has been done to create other sources of work. We don't have a single proper factory in the whole region. Just a beer factory, a cement factory and a noodle factory, and that's only because a Spanish businessman came and set one up. There's tourism but they spend all their money with a few agencies, in the centre of town. The rest of the city doesn't get anything. Within twenty years the

mines will be finished, the Cerro will collapse on top
of us, and the only thing left will be ruins.

One of the miners who arrived with the injured man comes
out of the hospital to move his van. He looks at us, gives a
thumbs-up and smiles. Apparently it's not serious.

* * *

'Sons of bitches!'

Pedro Villca hurls insults at three miners who appear
where two galleries meet, pushing a truck. They return the
insults and laugh. They've spent the morning shovelling
tons of rock and now they're going to take a break.

'This is Dominguito, the minister of the interior,' Villca
says, slapping one of the other miners on the back. Dominguito is tiny, a red-eyed veteran who smiles, displaying his
gappy teeth, stained green by coca leaves. 'We call him
the minister of the interior because he's spent thirty years
inside the mine.'

The three miners trudge along until they reach a large
cave, with copper and sulphur stalactites, the walls veined
with quartz, pyrite and tin. The light from their helmet
torches cuts through the stifling air.

The second miner is called Félix. His hands are covered
with grey mud. He squats down and washes them in a
puddle of *copajira*, the acidic water that accumulates in
the mines. Then he takes a few steps, turns to face the
wall, and pisses first on one hand then on the other.

'To get rid of the *copajira*, because it burns your skin,' explains Villca, amused at my astonishment.

Félix smiles and dries his hands on his trousers. He has almond eyes, high cheekbones, with the face of a naughty child who's been caught in the act, trapped between shame and pleasure. He doesn't say much. He came to the Potosí mine when he was twenty-three, two years ago, and at the beginning he only spoke Quechua and a few isolated words of Spanish. In his village, he herded cows, sheep and pigs, and his family grew potatoes, beans and wheat. But he is one of ten siblings and the family doesn't have enough land to support them all. Sometimes they went hungry.

'You get ill in the mine, but the money's good.'

When the *copajira* floods the galleries, the miners have to dig drainage channels. If they're not quick enough, the floor becomes swamped with mud, which then dries out, making the rails impassable for the trucks. At that point, the only solution is to break up the solid mud with a pickaxe, remove it with a shovel, and level the floor again.

'It's a bitch,' says Luis, the third miner. He's about forty years old, with great bags beneath his droopy eyes, and a trade unionist's moustache. 'Sometimes you have to change the rails, too, because the *copajira* bends them out of shape. Like our fingers!' he says. 'But the rails are old, it's like they're fused to the ground, changing them is hard. It's a bitch,' he repeats.

The miners take off their helmets, their boots, their vests, and they're left naked from the waist up. They're small and skinny, their torsos – like those of a bronze youth – widen at the chest, culminating in broad shoulders and muscular arms. They spread canvas sacks on the ground and lie down. They spit out the exhausted ball of coca leaves that they carry in their cheeks, rinse out their mouths with cold tea from a flask, and take fresh leaves from their plastic bags. They remove the central vein and pack the leaves into their mouths, along with some *yicta*, a pellet of plant ash which – when mixed with saliva – produces the chemical reaction that causes the leaves to release their alkaloids, including cocaine.

The rhythm of the work is dictated by the coca leaves: every three or four hours, as the wad of leaves begins to dry out and stops releasing stimulants, the miners spit it out and take a break.

'Coca takes away tiredness, hunger and thirst,' says Villca. 'It dulls your suffering. And warms your heart.'

Luis takes out a half-litre plastic bottle.

'*Quemapecho*,' he says – chest-burner – before taking a long swig and passing it on. The label reads: 'Guabirá: alcohol for human consumption. 96°. Great flavour.' The next miner drinks it neat then passes the bottle to me. I pretend to take a sip but barely even wet my lips. He laughs.

Coca, cigarettes and *quemapecho*: the fuel of the miners, keeping them working for six, seven or eight hours without so much as a scrap of food.

'Down here, the food gets contaminated. It's better not to eat,' Félix explains.

'Why worry about that? The silicosis will get you first,' replies Villca, and chuckles. Then he explains. 'After eight or ten years, the miner gets ill. If he's a cooperative member then he gets a pension. But sometimes the insurance company says it isn't silicosis, that he has to carry on working and then, when he dies, they do an autopsy, they remove lumps of ore from his lungs, like this' – he demonstrates – 'great handfuls of them.'

Sometimes a miner retires with silicosis; he doesn't show up at the mine again and people assume he's dead.

'One Sunday we travelled to Sucre, to watch Real Potosí play Universitario de Sucre. When we got inside the stadium, one of my comrades said: "Look over there, it's Juan, they told me he was dead!" And a bit farther away was another miner we thought was dead, and then another one, and another one ... When they retire they get sent to Sucre because it's lower down and the climate's better. They buy a little house and retire there. When we went to the stadium in Sucre it was packed with dead miners, all the dead miners were there supporting Real Potosí.'

'But some miners really disappear,' says Dominguito, the minister of the interior. 'When there's a big rockfall, it's impossible to find the bodies. Sometimes an arm appears and they take it away and bury it. Or a head.'

Villca, Luis and Dominguito share old stories, the kind that have been rolling around below the ground for decades – or centuries. Their younger colleague, Félix, listens as he kneads the coca leaves.

'Near here, a miner was crushed when a rock face collapsed,' says Dominguito. 'They found an arm sticking out from underneath. They couldn't get the body out so they cut off the arm and took it away to bury it.' He pauses for effect, then continues. 'A few days later, a driller is working on his own at night. Suddenly he hears noises. He goes to see who's wandering around the gallery and sees a miner, bent down, looking for something with his lamp. So he says: "What the fuck are you looking for?" And the miner stands up and he only has one arm. "I'm looking for my arm!" he replies. It was the dead man. The driller got the hell out of there. The next day, he went down with his comrades, and the dead man wasn't there any more. But right on that spot they found a really rich seam.'

'When there are ghosts in a gallery it means a seam's about to appear. That's what they say,' Villca explains. 'Down here there are bad galleries, where you hear voices. They say they're the voices of the dead, working in the night. You have to leave them in peace.'

I ask him if, perhaps, the voices might be due to the quantities of *quemapecho* that the miners drink.

'Ha! Yes. In the mine, we drink a lot,' says Dominiguito, and he laughs. 'You know, we get together with the Tío, we talk to him. In the mine, we say things that we don't say outside. Anything. The drink makes us angry, it makes us strong enough to work, it makes us fight. When we drink, we become like the Tío, we get angry and we fight.'

Dominguito came to Potosí when he was twelve. In his village, his family grew potatoes and reared some sheep and a few llamas, he says, but they were very poor. He came to the mine and he's spent his life down here, doing any job he was offered: breaking up rocks with a sledge-hammer, pushing the trucks through low tunnels, helping the driller.

'I've breathed in so much dust,' he says.

He clears his throat and coughs.

'Retiring is the worst thing you can do. Miners are used to the air down here, it gives us life, like the Tío giving you his breath, his energy, right? Outside, it's different. For the miners, the air outside isn't the same. The ones that stop working, that don't come back to the mine, they're the ones that die, right?'

Villca, an old miner, who swore to leave the mine because – at the age of fifty-nine – he'd already taken too many chances with death, pushes the wad of coca leaves against his cheek with his tongue, and looks at Dominguito without saying a word.

'These stories we tell,' Dominguito continues, smiling. 'After so many years in the mine, we belong to the Tío, we have his spirit in our blood, we're like a part of him, right?'

Two figures are cut into a section of smooth rock: coarse effigies of naked women, with huge breasts and gaping vaginas.

'And that? Who's the artist?'

They all laugh, and Dominguito explains.

'It's to make the Tío horny. So he'll fuck Pachamama and she'll give us the ore.'

* * *

'Just as, for Catholics, wine is the blood of Christ, for the miners hard liquor is the Tío's urine,' writes anthropologist Pascale Absi.

I remember the alcohol that Villca poured into the mouth of the Tío and which then gushed from the statue's penis.

When they're drunk, Absi argues, the miners are transformed. 'They become half-man, half-devil: they're not human any more. This notion of drunkenness cancels out all individual responsibility. Subject to the will of the Tío, the drunk miners are no longer deemed fully responsible for their actions.' The Tío is depicted with a huge erect penis and boundless sexual desire. Pachamama is the mountain, a woman whose seven skirts the miners must lift one by one, a woman they must penetrate with their drills to obtain the treasure within.

Absi records the testimony of a miner:

When the miner's a bit drunk, he kneels down in devotion, takes off his hat and says: 'Pachamama, I'm going to drill you. You give me what I'm after and I'll give you what you want. I'm going to lift up your skirt and stick the dynamite in, so give me your pussy.' I've never liked it when they talk like that, but that's the way the peasants' faith works. They're all riled up by the time they go into the mine, calling Pachamama a cunt, a fucking bitch; telling her to lift up her skirts so they can screw her. Pachamama chooses the one she wants. The first miner is looking for ore but he doesn't find it. Another miner comes along and hits a seam straight away. That's what happens. It's the same with a girl. It doesn't matter how much you want her, if she doesn't want you, you can't do a thing. And the more you trust your wife, just when you're least expecting it ...' (The miner makes the sign of the cuckold's horns with his fingers.) 'It's the same with the ore, it can abandon you at any moment.'

Inside the mine, Absi writes, the miners can transform themselves into a diabolical alter ego that possesses women. They are no longer themselves, they claim. It is the Tío, guiding their spirits.

* * *

Rosalía Aguilar is a guard at one of the Cerro Rico mine entrances, a miner's widow with seven children.

'In Pailaviri there was a young girl who sometimes worked in the mine, pushing trucks. Twenty years old. One time, she sat down to rest in the shaft and she fell asleep. She had a bad dream. She dreamed she was being raped, she woke up screaming, but there was nobody there. A few months went by and she realized she was pregnant. She gave birth to the *wawa* but the baby wasn't right. It had long pointy ears and people were scared of it. But the baby died soon. They said it was the Tío's baby, that the Tío has his way with any woman who enters the mine.'

* * *

Women can't enter the mine, say the miners, because the work is too hard, because they could have accidents and because they have to be protected against rape.

It's for their own good.

Absi explains that women formed a substantial part of the mining labour force during the colonial period, and also in the private sector during the twentieth century. She quotes statistics from 1917, when one in eight of those working in the mines of Potosí were women; and figures from 1950, when they were one in ten. Following the revolution in 1952, which nationalized the mines, the state mining company, Comibol, prohibited women from working below ground, although they continued to work outside, performing auxiliary tasks, breaking up rocks and so on. Now, the existence of small, private concessions means that a widow can inherit and work her husband's deposit, but social pressure is too strong and it's almost impossible to find a woman who actually does so. Absi records the case of two widows, Julia and Isabel, who used to wear trousers and worked side by side, extracting ore. The other miners marginalized them and were convinced they must be lesbians, that Julia was 'half man' because she was the one that handled the drill, and with this ambiguity they salvaged the notion that drilling was reserved for men.

With only a very few exceptions, widows renounce the claims of their dead husbands and accept the jobs the cooperatives offer them outside the mine, as guards and *palliris*.

The guards and the *palliris* earn between a sixth and a tenth of what the men earn in the mine.

Women can't enter the mine, say the men. It's for their own good.

*   *   *

Between 2020 and 2030, there will be no women in the senior ranks of the Bolivian army. At the moment, there is one female general and two colonels, but when they retire they will leave a gap. The officers' training academy barred women from entering in 1985 and didn't open its doors to them again until 2003. The women that were admitted in 2003 graduated in 2007, so it will be years before any of them reach the top.

When she turned seventeen, Alicia Quispe joined the army cadets. High school students can sign up and receive basic training at the barracks at weekends. The boys, who will have to do compulsory military service later on, are able to clock up some time without abandoning their studies. Although they don't have to do military service, increasing numbers of girls are also joining up: when the cadet force was established, around 20 per cent of recruits were girls, a figure that has gradually risen to 40 per cent.

Alicia is sitting with her mother, her sister, her aunt and her cousins at a table in a fried chicken restaurant. She's wearing olive-green fatigues, black boots and a green cap with a wide peak that comes down almost over her eyes. She has a patch with the Bolivian flag sewn to her right sleeve, her surname QUISPE embroidered on one breast pocket, and the word EJERCITO, army, on the other.

She submitted her school grades to the barracks, they gave her a medical check-up and today she got her uniform. In the restaurant, she's ordered a bottle of beer. Alicia's aunt takes photos with her phone, while Alicia laughs and tells her to stop. When the staff call out their order, Alicia is the one who gets up and walks across the restaurant to collect the trays of chicken and chips, watched by the customers at the other tables.

She starts to eat the fried chicken and says she wants to do her cadet service but she's not sure if she's going to join the army afterwards.

'I don't know if I want to. Women didn't used to be allowed to.'

* * *

It's hard to say goodbye. I'm leaving Bolivia, taking everything I can – the time, knowledge and trust that people have given me; the raw materials for a book – and the suspicion that the book won't do them any good. Bolivia is also one of those countries that is an exporter of sensational stories: journalists, writers, film-makers, photographers, anthropologists and storytellers come here in search of tales of poverty and violence, which look great when we get home but won't benefit the protagonists of these stories in any way.

It's hard to say goodbye to Alicia, Rosa and Evelyn, because this is when I start to worry. Will this book help them at all? Will it help anyone? Will it help to talk about the mechanisms of injustice and those who benefit from it? It's hard because these thoughts take me home, back to my desk, when I'm still saying goodbye on the *canchamina*.

My farewell – to this journey, to this book – is clumsy.

On my last evening in Potosí I go up the hill to the hut where Alicia, Rosa and Evelyn live. I have printed off some of the photos I've taken over the past few weeks, we take some more photos, have something to eat, and exchange phone numbers (with which, I discover later, we will be unable to communicate). I know that the doctor has recommended a scan for Rosa to identify whether her headaches are due to a tumour but that she hasn't had the scan because she doesn't have any health insurance or the 130 dollars it would cost. I manage to find a moment alone with Alicia to discuss the matter. I go round and round in explanations and she nods wordlessly, because she doesn't need to say anything: up here on the *canchamina* this prudishness about money is my privilege.

Alicia will go back to the mine. She's already told me. She's joined the cadets and she'll continue with her studies and tell her teachers and the staff at the NGOs that she doesn't go down the mine any more. But she will. They pay her forty pesos for every night she spends pushing trucks. She's one of the few people on Cerro Rico who imagines a different life for herself and who struggles to achieve it, and nobody is going to change her mind. She tells me she's going to demand the same pay as the miners who do the same work.

I leave Alicia on the *canchamina*, next to the rails that lead into the dark mouth of the mountain. Tonight, she'll enter the mine.

BIBLIOGRAPHY

Absi, Pascale. *Los ministros del diablo. El trabajo y sus representaciones en las minas de Potosí*. Fundación PIEB, La Paz, 2005

Albarracín, Juan. *El Superestado minero y el derrumbe de la oligarquía boliviana*. Plural Editores, La Paz, 2008

Anderson, Jon Lee. *Che Guevara. A revolutionary life*. Grove Press, New York, 1997

Arancibia-Andrade, Freddy. *Uncía. Historia, poesía, cuentos, turismo*. Norte Potosí, 2008

Arzáns de Orsúa y Vela, Bartolomé. *Relatos de la Villa Imperial de Potosí*. Plural Editores, La Paz, 2009

Baptista Gumucio, Mariano. *El mundo desde Potosí. Vida y reflexiones de Bartolomé Arzáns de Orsúa y Vela (1676–1736)*. Garza Azul, La Paz, 2001

Céspedes, Augusto. *Metal del Diablo*. Editora Juventud, La Paz, 1998

Crespo, Arturo. *El rostro minero de Bolivia*. La Paz, 2009

De Mesa, José; De Mesa Gisbert, Carlos; Gisbert, Teresa. *Historia de Bolivia*. Editorial Gisbert, La Paz, 2008

Escóbar, Filemón. *De la revolución al pachacuti*. Garza Azul, La Paz, 2008

Escóbar, Filemón. *El Evangelio es la encarnación de los derechos humanos*. Plural Editores, La Paz, 2011

Espinoza, Jorge. *Minería boliviana. Su realidad*. Plural Editores, La Paz, 2010

Fernández, Luis Alfonso. *La Real Casa de la Moneda*. Los Amigos del Libro, La Paz, 1979

Ferrufino, Rubén; Eróstegui, Rodolfo; Gavincha, Marco. *Potosí. El Cerro nuestro de cada día. Relevancia económica en la región y ciudad capital*. Ediciones Labor, La Paz, 2011

Flores, Juan Pablo. *Desarrollo, equidad y progreso de Bolivia*. Observatorio Boliviano de los Recursos Naturales, El Alto, 2009

Francescone, Kirsten; Díaz, Vladimir. *Cooperativas mineras: entre socios, patrones y peones*. Petropress, Cochabamba, 2012

González Pazos, Jesús. *Bolivia. La construcción de un país indígena*. Icaria, Barcelona, 2007

Iriarte, Gregorio. *Análisis crítico de la realidad*. Grupo Editorial Kipus, Cochabamba, 2007

Iriarte, Gregorio. *Narcotráfico y política. Militarismo y mafia en Bolivia*. Latin America Bureau–Iepala Editorial, Bolivia, 1982

Klein, Naomi. *The Shock Doctrine*. Penguin Press, London, 2008

LIDEMA (Liga de Defensa del Medio Ambiente). *Cantumarca, población precolombina de Potosí afectada por la actividad minera*. Potosí, 2008

LIDEMA (Liga de Defensa del Medio Ambiente). *Investigaciones socioambientales 2009–2010*. Potosí, 2011

Mendoza, Jaime. *En las tierras del Potosí*. Ediciones Puerta del Sol, La Paz, 1973

Michard, Jocelyn. *Cooperativas mineras en Bolivia*. CEDIB, Cochabamba, 2008

Ministerio de Economía y Finanzas Públicas. *Memoria de la Economía Boliviana*. La Paz, 2012

Molina, Cecilia. *Un horizonte al final del socavón. Programa de acción para la eliminación del trabajo infantil minero en Siglo XX*. International Labour Organization, Llallagua, 2003

Museo Nacional de Arte. *Supay. Los caminos del* Tío. La Paz, 2011

NATS. *Memoria del I y II encuentro local de Nats*. Cepromin–Terre des Hommes, Llallagua, 2006

Nooteboom, Cees. *Nomad's Hotel*. Harvill Secker, London, 2006

Poppe, René. *Interior mina*. Plural Editores, La Paz, 2003

Poveda, Pablo. *Formas de producción de las cooperativas mineras de Bolivia*. Cedla, La Paz, 2014

Querejazu Calvo, Roberto. *Llallagua, trono del rey del estaño*. Los Amigos del Libro, La Paz–Cochabamba, 1998

Quiroga Santa Cruz, Marcelo. *El saqueo de Bolivia*. Ediciones Puerta del Sol, La Paz, 1973

Reid, Michael. *Forgotten Continent*. Yale University Press, New Haven, 2009

Bibliography

Rocha Monroy, Ramón. *Potosí 1600*. Alfaguara, La Paz, 2002

Sachs, Jeffrey D. *The End of Poverty*. Penguin Press, New York, 2005

Sánchez-Ostiz, Miguel. *Cuaderno boliviano*. Alberdania, Irún, 2008

Taboada Terán, Néstor. *El precio del estaño*. Plural Editores, La Paz, 2006

Tapia, Rosario. *Minería y conflictos socioambientales en Cantumarca*. Fundación PIEB, Potosí, 2010

UDAPE (Unidad de Análisis de Políticas Sociales y Económicas). *Sexto informe de progreso de los Objetivos de Desarrollo del Milenio en Bolivia*. La Paz, 2010

UNDP (United Nations Development Programme). *Informes sobre Desarrollo Humano en Bolivia*. New York, 2010, 2011, 2012 and 2013

Viezzer, Moema; Barrios de Chungara, Domitila (tr. Victoria Ortiz). *Let me speak!* Monthly Review Press, New York, 1978

Ziegler, Jean. *El odio a Occidente*. Ediciones Península, Barcelona, 2010

JUN 1 4 2019

ZED

Zed is a platform for marginalised voices across the globe.

It is the world's largest publishing collective and a world leading example of alternative, non-hierarchical business practice.

It has no CEO, no MD and no bosses and is owned and managed by its workers who are all on equal pay.

It makes its content available in as many languages as possible.

It publishes content critical of oppressive power structures and regimes.

It publishes content that changes its readers' thinking.

It publishes content that other publishers won't and that the establishment finds threatening.

It has been subject to repeated acts of censorship by states and corporations.

It fights all forms of censorship.

It is financially and ideologically independent of any party, corporation, state or individual.

Its books are shared all over the world.

www.zedbooks.net

@ZedBooks